# Contents

*Page*

# List of tables

# List of figures

# Summary and conclusions

**The problem**

- Certain estates have concentrated on them large numbers of vulnerable and poor families. Levels of crime there are several times the national average. Deprivation and social disorganisation are acute. The danger of a downward spiral of social disintegration and violence are endemic. From time to time such estates erupt to gain national media attention. They are then forgotten by the media and the public at large. Such areas encapsulate the most intractable problems of housing, crime and social policy more generally.

- Structural economic and labour market changes and limited economic opportunities in some communities form the background to the plight of many of these areas. Housing policy cannot, on its own, match or counter these forces. Nor can it simply abandon those who are caught in their consequences.

**Response**

- Previous research identified weak and over centralised local authority housing management and poor maintenance as major additional factors helping to drive vulnerable communities to the verge of disaster or worse.

- In the 1980s the Department of the Environment targeted certain estates and encouraged the local authorities to introduce decentralised, estate based housing management which involved tenants in the management of their environment. This approach has been particularly associated with the Priority Estates Project funded by the Department.

- Though it was argued that this approach improved housing standards and tenant satisfaction, this had not been independently tested nor had the claim that such intervention could have a secondary impact on crime.

**The research**

- In collaboration with the Home Office, the Department of the Environment sponsored an independent experiment to test the impact of this policy on both the standards of the housing service and levels of crime. Two experimental estates were chosen, one in Tower Hamlets and one in Hull, on which the full PEP approach was attempted. These were matched with two control estates in the same local authority areas on which such an approach was not to be tried. In practice, it was impossible to prevent these control areas adopting some element of decentralised management during the research period, but not to the same extent as the local offices on the experimental estates.

- The research was designed to answer three questions:

    (i)   How far is it possible to decentralise local housing department functions to an estate level and what are the barriers to that process?

    (ii)  What impact does such a strategy have on the quality of the housing service provided, on the quality of the physical environment, on tenant satisfaction and the attractiveness of the estate to prospective tenants ?

(iii)   What are the links between a changed housing environment, if it is achieved, a more active staff presence, tenant involvement and the extent of informal social controls and the level of crime ?

This report is primarily concerned with the first two questions. That part of the research focusing on the impact on crime is reported in a separate publication by the Home Office.

- The chosen research design was a small scale but very intensive social experiment. The field work was conducted over a three year period from June 1987 to June 1990.

- A wide range of research instruments were used:

  - a household interview with tenants before the management changes, repeated afterwards;

  - interviews with staff;

  - performance indicators derived from local authority records;

  - indicators of environmental nuisances such as broken doors, blocked waste chutes, graffiti and rubbish. A photographic record;

  - regular interviews with local officials and housing staff.

These methods are described in detail in the report.

**The process**
Estate based offices

- Offices that were accessible to tenants and provided a comprehensive housing management service were opened on the experimental estates, though there was some resistance to the devolution of some functions in London.

- The advantages of having staff present on the estate were evident from close observation. Out of order lifts were reported quickly. Poor cleaning, squatters and various nuisances were reported readily. The estate officers knew their estates well. Workmen coming into the office could get ready access to property when they needed to. Such small practical matters added up to a more responsive and effective housing management and maintenance process.

- The office staff modified the PEP model to suit local circumstances introducing specialist functions within the teams. A minimum of five, and preferably 7-8 management staff, seemed to work best in any one office with supporting repairs staff, caretakers and clerical staff. The staff ratio suggested by PEP of one officer to 350 properties proved appropriate but even at that level staff on the most difficult estate could be stretched.

- In the office that worked best there was:

  - One team leader who ran the office, was responsible for the staff, tenant liaison and links with other services as well as the estate office budget.

  - Two neighbourhood housing assistants responsible for rent arrears, voids and tenant relations more generally.

- Two staff combined the functions of reception, repairs reporting, secretarial and administrative work. When extra properties were added to the estate an extra advice and reception worker was taken on. A housing benefit adviser came into the office on one afternoon a week in April 1990.

- Four caretakers covered the 7 blocks on the estate and one handyman did odd jobs around the estate and attempted to keep the unadopted roads and open spaces free of litter and rubbish.

- The direct labour repairs team, and later a private contractor repairs team, had an office adjacent to the estate office and worked closely with it.

## Tenant involvement

● After three years of intensive work in Hull, PEP had set up a solid base of tenant involvement, though it had failed to get its full preferred model of an Estate Management Board in place.

● In Tower Hamlets less progress was made in general tenant involvement. The exception was a successful initiative to setting up what proved to be an effective Bengali tenants' group.

## The outcomes
### Tenants' attitudes

● The greatest dissatisfaction had been expressed by tenants in Hull. In 1987 61% of tenants on the experimental estate thought conditions had got worse in the previous two or three years. After the experiment with estate based management and partial environmental changes only 38% thought the estate had got worse and 27% thought there had been improvement, a view expressed by only 3% three years before. On the control estate 79% thought things had stayed the same or got worse and 9% did not know what to say.

● In London, tenants on both experimental and control estates thought improvements had taken place. The experimental estate showed the most progress. On the experimental estate 51% thought the estate had improved compared with 29% on the control.

### Environment

● A detailed survey of environmental nuisance scores through the research period showed a 30% improvement in the scores on the London experimental estate by the end of the research.

● Very little change was observed on the London control estate, except in the block on which major environmental work was undertaken.

● In Hull, the part of the experimental estate on which environmental work had been undertaken, showed striking improvement. In contrast, one block and a nearby area into which formerly homeless and vulnerable young people had been moved showed a very sharp deterioration. The control estate showed virtually no change.

● The deterioration in an otherwise improving area dramatically illustrated the importance of allocations policy and wider issues of housing vulnerable and homeless young people.

## Repairs management

● Local ordering of repairs from the local offices proved very successful especially on one experimental estate. Sharp increases in the number of jobs ordered followed as tenants found the system responded. This did not happen on the control estate.

- The local repairs teams were shown to be very effective in getting more work done more quickly.

- Repairs work improved on all the estates in the period in response to competitive tendering and other factors but decentralisation also had a significant additional effect.

- Longer term repairs strategies were less effective, not least because of cash constraints, but also because of the legacy of past neglect.

**Allocations and empty property**

- Devolved responsibility and a clear focus by the local teams on voids control did reduce the number of empty properties significantly on both experimental and control estates in London. The greater speed of letting on the experimental estate reflected the fact that officers were on the spot.

- The key factor that worked in the opposite direction in Hull was an allocations policy which led to the placing of vulnerable single people in blocks of flats with the adverse consequences referred to above.

**Rent arrears**

- Estate office based rent collection on lines advocated by PEP was never fully implemented in the experimental sites which made it difficult to draw any conclusions. However, one experimental estate did show less of an increase in rent arrears after the changes in housing benefit rules. This may have been related to the local office and housing benefit advice but the evidence is inconclusive.

**Capital programme**

- In Hull, a well prepared capital investment programme was slowly coming to fruition. The programme of tenant consultation had been excellent but the pace of completion, relying on employment trainees, was slow. The capital programme on the Tower Hamlets estates was slow and poorly organised.

**Crime**

- The underlying goal of the joint research project was to test how far the improvements in housing services, tenant involvement and design could impact on crime.

- The research demonstrated the importance of underlying social factors as well as the contribution estate based housing services could have.

- Rates of victimisation on the London experimental estate declined significantly but improvements on the other estate were greater. Capital work to improve the security of a block of flats had taken place on the control estate but the same kind of work had not been completed on the experimental estate. The difference may also reflect the active local tenant activity that took place on the control estate.

- In Hull there was a significant decrease in burglary on the experimental estate relative to the control. Fear of crime also fell. However, person related crime and disruption on one part of the estate grew. This related to the changed allocations policy and the concentration of young people that resulted which is described above.

- A detailed account of the impact on crime is given in the Home Office report.

**Conclusions**

Overall, the evidence from the experimental and control estates in this study does support the hypothesis that estate based management tends to improve the standards of housing service and the quality of life of the tenants.

The decentralisation of housing management and maintenance functions to an estate level did succeed in improving the standard of most aspects of the housing service, most notably short term repairs, and raised tenant satisfaction. It was also associated with a reduced level of property damage and nuisance.

To be fully effective in the wider objectives of community building and informal social control, however, tenant involvement was critical. This was only achieved to varying degrees on the two estates. Where it was most successful the PEP advisers had played a major part.

If tenant involvement is to be taken seriously on this kind of estate it involves significant management attention at senior level. Work with tenants is a time consuming and skilled task. It cannot simply be tacked onto a busy housing manager's role. It has to be built into the job definition and properly resourced. Training is also important. The level of responsibility put onto the estate managers, their sense of isolation from the centre, their high profile interaction with tenants, for which they had not been fully prepared, their pivotal role with other agencies, not least the police, all emphasised the need for good initial training and above all for **regular** staff development and training and senior management support.

The limits to any attempts to improve the long term quality of life and vulnerability to crime on such estates are also evident from this study.

The stresses of poverty and unemployment have been added to by Government policies, of all parties, that have reduced the scale of institutional care and shelter for vulnerable people. In that situation people in the greatest housing need , who are desperate for accommodation, naturally find their way to the least desirable properties on the least desired estates. Such situations occur most often on public housing estates since the authorities have an obligation to house those who meet the criteria of the homeless persons legislation.

If the more successful families exercise their power to exit from these poor communities **and** those that remain are left to carry the task of accommodating society's most vulnerable people, because no one else will, it should be no surprise that the fragile ties that barely hold the social fabric together disintegrate.

First, housing authorities must be sensitive enough to prevent the undue concentration of at risk individuals.

Second, because this will never entirely succeed, the housing management function must be enlarged to include the task of mobilising support to sustain those individuals and the social fabric of at risk estates.

Where the situation is seen to be deteriorating, and preferably before it does so, wider intervention will be necessary. The local estate based manager would be the key agent in alerting other agencies. The estate office, if it exists, is the centre of intelligence and tenant contact, or should be. Responsibility for coordinating other agencies' work would have to lie with a task force kept as informal and flexible as possible. Job opportunities, the local economy and transport links may prove critical.

Training programmes for housing managers should recognise the need to take account of the inter agency, inter disciplinary nature of the housing management function.

In short, estate based management is a necessary but not a sufficient condition for combating housing and social decay on deprived housing estates.

*Part One*

# Deprivation and Housing Management: Diagnosis and Response

# Chapter 1

# Defining the problem of problem estates

1.1 The origins of the Priority Estates Project (PEP) are, in their way, a classic example of social administration at work. They lie partly in research and policy development undertaken within the Department of the Environment (DoE) itself, partly in the insight of individuals working in the front line responding to social situations as they saw them, but above all they lie in the profound social and economic changes that were occurring in the late 1970s and 1980s.

1.2 As the extreme housing shortages of the earlier decades began to recede and owner occupation came within the reach of more families, local authorities began to find difficulty in letting their most unpopular housing stock.

1.3 In fact there was nothing new about the unpopularity of certain estates nor the concentration of social deprivation on them. Teachers and social workers had long complained of the effects of "dump estates" and evidence of the hard to let nature of some blocks can be found in the minutes of the LCC Housing Department even before the first World War (Power 1987). What was new was the scale and nature of the phenomenon. Different participants in the housing market saw the issue differently. For central government, press reports of empty council property were evidence of wasted economic resources. For local authorities, it meant financial and political embarrassment. For tenants, if anyone concerned themselves with them, it meant a decline in the standard of life in what was often already an unattractive environment.

**A DoE initiative**

1.4 Local authority returns to the Department showing the scale of hard to let housing in 1974 convinced the DoE that it should take action. The Housing Directorate initiated a study by its own research section of 30 hard to let estates, as defined by the local housing departments. The research team which was composed of social scientists and architects undertook its initial fieldwork in 1976-7. There followed seminars with local authorities at which the team presented their preliminary results, but they were not actually published until 1981 (DoE 1981a, 1981b, 1981c).

1.5 The report was admirably forthright. Obviously shocked by the scale of physical neglect they observed and the concentration of poor social conditions on some estates, the team concluded that the "hard to let" label was a misnomer. What they were really observing was merely the most unattractive end of the public housing market. They were the tip of a much larger problem of poor housing management. The surveys described in vivid detail, supported by photographs, the physical conditions and some of the social consequences for the tenants. They also described the steps the local authorities were taking to remedy the situation.

1.6 These were of two kinds - architectural improvements, often undertaken without any consultation, and a change in allocation policies. The intention was to cease to allocate large families or single parent families to tower blocks on estates with high concentrations of such families. Some authorities combined this with a policy of moving off the estate those they viewed as problem families. In a few places a community development worker had been employed and, experimentally, in a very few a single estate officer was employed to get at least some recognisable housing department presence onto the estates.

1.7    The DoE team concluded that capital works on their own would be inadequate. A mixed approach was necessary. They put as their first priority a change in the quality of housing management. They commended the idea of employing housing staff on the estates - caretakers and an estate officer - and they stressed the important role that a community worker could play, at least initially, in turning an estate round and in finding out what changes tenants wanted. Coordination of all the elements in the housing service was needed. However, the idea of a localised housing service was expressed in an extremely rudimentary form. It was not clear who was to do what or how a single estate officer was meant to cope with the scale of problems involved nor how the "coordination" advocated was to occur or at what level. There was no analysis of how the management weaknesses had arisen in the first place.

1.8    The underlying causal analysis appeared to be that

1. the size of the estates made them difficult to manage;

2. their architectural features often added to the difficulty;

3. problem tenants were either allocated to or found their way onto such estates because no one else wanted them, adding yet again to the management task.

More and better management of a somewhat ill defined kind was therefore necessary on these priority estates. Despite the lack of prescriptive precision this was a very important step forward by central government, moving as it was into an area of work previously left entirely to local authorities.

**The priority estates project is born**

Phase One 1979 - 1984

1.9    The DoE wished to develop and test these ideas further. It proposed setting up three pilot projects with three experimental estates each managed locally by a consultant employed out of project funds. Three women with experience of local housing work were taken on.

1.10    Ann Blaber came from the Safe Neighbourhoods Unit, a group set up by NACRO, the National Association for the Care and Resettlement of Offenders. As part of its work on crime prevention it had concluded that certain estates were proving a fertile breeding ground for crime. It was unconvinced that architectural design was the prime cause, as some had suggested (Newman 1972; Wilson 1978; 1980). An important element in prevention required work with tenants helping to rebuild informal social controls that existed in more stable communities. NACRO had begun work on a heavily vandalised estate in Widnes in 1976 and went on to create its Safe Neighbourhoods Unit to develop this approach. Its strategy was to work with tenants "planning improvements in such a way that they will feel inclined to maintain and protect them" (NACRO 1982).

1.11    Lesley Andrews, while in the Department of the Environment, had studied tenants' attitudes to their local authority landlords. Her research had shown how alienated tenants were from the town hall and the distant housing departments. Caretaking was poor, lifts did not work, tenants felt alienated both from their landlords and their local community and a spiral of decline set in (Andrews 1979).

1.12   Anne Power had worked with community groups and housing cooperatives in Islington.

1.13   These three women were to work on three estates developing the ideas that had sprung from the initial research. The overall project was given the title, the Priority Estates Project. It was only later that it became a broader Departmental initiative. The two initial projects were in Hackney and Bolton. When the Conservative Government came to power in 1979 the future of the project and indeed the research function of the Department was reviewed and it was decided to cut the period of the project from five to three years. The research was subsequently extended to the full five years. The original third project, on which Anne Power had been recruited to work, was cut out but, since she was already under contract, she was given a roving commission to advise councils throughout the country on measures to rescue hard to let or deprived estates. She insisted that to do that work properly she needed to be working intensively on an estate of her own. With the collaboration of the GLC she ran a project that later became a PEP project on the Tulse Hill estate in south London. Anne Power visited about sixty authorities in this period.

1.14   The essence of the group's philosophy at this time was to encourage the opening of a local estate office on each estate and to involve and consult tenants.

1.15   In 1983/4 the Department of the Environment undertook a review of progress on the two original estates on which intensive work was being done with the two consultants and of the other authorities with whom Anne Power was working. Household surveys in 1979 and 1984 on the two original estates suggested that tenant satisfaction and tenant turnover had improved. Anne Power had also found that several authorities had already developed strategies to cope with problem estates which shared some or many of the approaches the team were advocating. The results were combined and all the evidence pulled together in the report, *Local Housing Management* (DoE 1984) which was sent to all local authorities. PEP was funded for three more years to work with nine projects, two in Wales.

Phase Two 1984-7

1.16   By this time the team's prescriptive model had become much more detailed - what functions should be undertaken in each office, the number of properties it should serve and the importance of a devolved estate budget.

1.17   PEP had developed its own very coherent philosophy. The reasons for this lie in the motivations and origins of the group of consultants recruited in the early 1980s and of the DoE researchers who developed the model. We saw that Anne Blaber had come from NACRO and had seen tenant involvement and local management as a response to high crime rates and the collapse of informal social control. Anne Power explained her early experience in rather similar terms. Her initial involvement with the Holloway Tenants' Cooperative had come about because of plans to demolish an area of sound housing which had been purchased by the council prior to demolition. She saw the area spiralling downwards with local services rapidly deteriorating. The area was being effectively abandoned, as council staff felt it pointless or too dangerous to operate in the area. What she saw reminded her vividly of her experience in Chicago. In her view, housing decline was merely a part of that process but it was the point through which a reversal of the spiral had to be attempted. Community development workers operating in a vacuum, unrelated to realistic service objectives, were counter productive. She therefore concluded that tenant involvement in achieving practical service goals was the right approach. Only if service improvements were achieved could the spiral of decline be checked and tenants given confidence to achieve larger change. Thus her perspective from the outset was wider than that of the housing service alone.

1.18   The detailed PEP model developed out of the consultants' day to day experience on their estates. The pre war GLC estate in south London on which Anne Power was working, for example, was on the point of social disintegration, a large proportion of the properties were empty, there was widespread squatting and burglary, and virtually no housing service remained. She persuaded the GLC to let her experiment with an estate office, local lettings, caretaking and repairs. Many of her ideas were formulated during this period. The local lettings speeded the process and reduced the number of empty properties dramatically. When the GLC was abolished, the estate reverted to the local authority which abandoned the estate based approach and many of the old problems began to re-emerge.

1.19   It was this experience that convinced Anne Power that all the main landlord functions had to be concentrated in a very accessible local office.

**The diagnosis**

1.20   PEP's diagnosis of the deficiencies of local authority housing management is best expounded in *Property Before People* (Power 1987) and in *Is Public Housing Manageable?* (Power 1988).

1.21   The diagnosis falls into two parts. The first concerns the emergence of hard to let estates and the spiral of social malaise into which they fall. The second deals with the decline in the managerial effectiveness of local authority housing departments.

1.22   Power argued that the phenomenon of social polarisation in housing was not new. Drawing on records of housing authorities earlier in the century and from Octavia Hill's work she found a remarkable continuity and similarity in the social processes at work, whoever the landlord. In the nineteen thirties, when local authorities had been confined almost exclusively to rehousing from slum clearance the problem had become acute and had then, as in the 1970's, become a focus for central government concern (CHAC 1939). For much of the period after the Second World War, council housing had been something of a privilege conferred on long term local residents while private landlords continued to cater for many of the poorest groups. Even so there had always been less desirable property and it was allocated to the less desirable and most difficult tenants. This had been a basic principle of housing management in the public sector. It reflected both a moral position and a practical need. As housing managers saw it, it was unfair that tenants who could not look after their property or were a nuisance to their neighbours, should be allocated to the better property. Moreover, the promise of better housing to good tenants was an incentive to good behaviour that managers needed to be able to keep good order and maintain property on their estates. This led naturally to the most marginal groups being allocated to the worst estates and to the " best" tenants moving on. At the same time better situated people on the waiting lists could afford to hold on and wait until places on more desirable estates became available. Thus demand and supply factors had always been at work but in the 1970's and 1980's both intensified. Growing owner occupation was removing from the public sector pool of tenants precisely the group of most stable, property conscious households that had been the strongest elements on the early post war estates. These exit factors were reinforced by entry factors too.

1.12   Anne Power had worked with community groups and housing cooperatives in Islington.

1.13   These three women were to work on three estates developing the ideas that had sprung from the initial research. The overall project was given the title, the Priority Estates Project. It was only later that it became a broader Departmental initiative. The two initial projects were in Hackney and Bolton. When the Conservative Government came to power in 1979 the future of the project and indeed the research function of the Department was reviewed and it was decided to cut the period of the project from five to three years. The research was subsequently extended to the full five years. The original third project, on which Anne Power had been recruited to work, was cut out but, since she was already under contract, she was given a roving commission to advise councils throughout the country on measures to rescue hard to let or deprived estates. She insisted that to do that work properly she needed to be working intensively on an estate of her own. With the collaboration of the GLC she ran a project that later became a PEP project on the Tulse Hill estate in south London. Anne Power visited about sixty authorities in this period.

1.14   The essence of the group's philosophy at this time was to encourage the opening of a local estate office on each estate and to involve and consult tenants.

1.15   In 1983/4 the Department of the Environment undertook a review of progress on the two original estates on which intensive work was being done with the two consultants and of the other authorities with whom Anne Power was working. Household surveys in 1979 and 1984 on the two original estates suggested that tenant satisfaction and tenant turnover had improved. Anne Power had also found that several authorities had already developed strategies to cope with problem estates which shared some or many of the approaches the team were advocating. The results were combined and all the evidence pulled together in the report, *Local Housing Management* (DoE 1984) which was sent to all local authorities. PEP was funded for three more years to work with nine projects, two in Wales.

Phase Two 1984-7

1.16   By this time the team's prescriptive model had become much more detailed - what functions should be undertaken in each office, the number of properties it should serve and the importance of a devolved estate budget.

1.17   PEP had developed its own very coherent philosophy. The reasons for this lie in the motivations and origins of the group of consultants recruited in the early 1980s and of the DoE researchers who developed the model. We saw that Anne Blaber had come from NACRO and had seen tenant involvement and local management as a response to high crime rates and the collapse of informal social control. Anne Power explained her early experience in rather similar terms. Her initial involvement with the Holloway Tenants' Cooperative had come about because of plans to demolish an area of sound housing which had been purchased by the council prior to demolition. She saw the area spiralling downwards with local services rapidly deteriorating. The area was being effectively abandoned, as council staff felt it pointless or too dangerous to operate in the area. What she saw reminded her vividly of her experience in Chicago. In her view, housing decline was merely a part of that process but it was the point through which a reversal of the spiral had to be attempted. Community development workers operating in a vacuum, unrelated to realistic service objectives, were counter productive. She therefore concluded that tenant involvement in achieving practical service goals was the right approach. Only if service improvements were achieved could the spiral of decline be checked and tenants given confidence to achieve larger change. Thus her perspective from the outset was wider than that of the housing service alone.

1.18   The detailed PEP model developed out of the consultants' day to day experience on their estates. The pre war GLC estate in south London on which Anne Power was working, for example, was on the point of social disintegration, a large proportion of the properties were empty, there was widespread squatting and burglary, and virtually no housing service remained. She persuaded the GLC to let her experiment with an estate office, local lettings, caretaking and repairs. Many of her ideas were formulated during this period. The local lettings speeded the process and reduced the number of empty properties dramatically. When the GLC was abolished, the estate reverted to the local authority which abandoned the estate based approach and many of the old problems began to re-emerge.

1.19   It was this experience that convinced Anne Power that all the main landlord functions had to be concentrated in a very accessible local office.

**The diagnosis**

1.20   PEP's diagnosis of the deficiencies of local authority housing management is best expounded in *Property Before People* (Power 1987) and in *Is Public Housing Manageable?* (Power 1988).

1.21   The diagnosis falls into two parts. The first concerns the emergence of hard to let estates and the spiral of social malaise into which they fall. The second deals with the decline in the managerial effectiveness of local authority housing departments.

1.22   Power argued that the phenomenon of social polarisation in housing was not new. Drawing on records of housing authorities earlier in the century and from Octavia Hill's work she found a remarkable continuity and similarity in the social processes at work, whoever the landlord. In the nineteen thirties, when local authorities had been confined almost exclusively to rehousing from slum clearance the problem had become acute and had then,as in the 1970's, become a focus for central government concern (CHAC 1939). For much of the period after the Second World War, council housing had been something of a privilege conferred on long term local residents while private landlords continued to cater for many of the poorest groups. Even so there had always been less desirable property and it was allocated to the less desirable and most difficult tenants. This had been a basic principle of housing management in the public sector. It reflected both a moral position and a practical need. As housing managers saw it, it was unfair that tenants who could not look after their property or were a nuisance to their neighbours, should be allocated to the better property. Moreover, the promise of better housing to good tenants was an incentive to good behaviour that managers needed to be able to keep good order and maintain property on their estates. This led naturally to the most marginal groups being allocated to the worst estates and to the " best" tenants moving on. At the same time better situated people on the waiting lists could afford to hold on and wait until places on more desirable estates became available. Thus demand and supply factors had always been at work but in the 1970's and 1980's both intensified. Growing owner occupation was removing from the public sector pool of tenants precisely the group of most stable, property conscious households that had been the strongest elements on the early post war estates. These exit factors were reinforced by entry factors too.

Pressure, not least from central government (CHAC 1969), led authorities to open their property to more recent residents, to the homeless and to those no longer able to stay in various forms of institutional care. The Housing (Homeless Persons) Act 1977, had required local authorities to house families with children, both increasing the demand from such families and reducing the effective sanctions that could be brought to bear if they proved difficult tenants.

1.23    The second and most original element in Power's diagnosis was her account of what had happened to the housing management function in local authorities in the twentieth century. Local authorities had been so affected by the financial and political rewards of building new houses that they had given little attention to managing their property. The interlocking functions of a landlord came to be undertaken by discrete existing departments within the authorities. The finance department collected the rents, the works or direct labour section did the repairs, the parks department the open spaces and so on. Even when these functions were amalgamated under one Housing Department roof the functional separation continued. So, too, did the process of centralisation for reasons of supposed efficiency. No one could therefore be held responsible for the situation on any one estate. Nor was there any one to whom tenants could turn or complain. The historical account of how this happened is one of the most convincing parts of the argument. It is out of this analysis that PEP'S prescriptions for change arose. In some ways, however, the diagnosis could have been pushed still further. It is largely consistent with modern theories of large scale organisations and with the economics of public bureaucracies. The pattern of evolution described reflects the fact that officials and politicians were reacting in entirely rational ways to the incentive structures that faced them, as were tenants to the housing market outside. It seems rational for an individual housing manager to use the reward of better housing to encourage tenants to act in socially responsible ways, and not to spend his or her limited time working closely with particular families which would increase the stress of the job. The wish to work in a specialised team in a central department away from the day to day pressures is also understandable.

1.24    In the same way the process of social polarisation described reflects the logic of a successfully differentiated housing market. Housing consumers want to live alongside "good " neighbours, house prices reflect perceptions of the neighbourhood, as much as, or more than, the physical nature of the property. The more scope there is for these preferences to be reflected in the housing market the more problematic will be tenures that serve the bottom end of the income and social structure. The same consumer preferences are reflected in the public sector whether there is a formal cash market or not. The "problems" perceived at the bottom of the market are really, it may be argued, just a reflection of the "successes" at the other end of the market. Thus the forces at work may be even more powerful than Power admitted in her original thesis. Any successful competitive market for a "positional good" (Hirsch 1979), which housing is to a significant extent, is likely to produce a residuum and all the social costs that go with that, of which crime and social disintegration in the areas concerned, are merely part. Is there any solution?

**The prescription**

1.25    The idea that it was possible to reverse a cycle of bureaucratic decline drew directly on Jane Jacobs' book, *The Economy of Cities*.

1.26    Jacobs (1970) had argued, from United States experience, that large urban bureaucracies had an inherent tendency to expand but in the end they

7

became so inefficient that units broke away, attracted good staff, undermined the old central bureaucracies, and took on a life of their own. This began a virtuous cycle of regeneration. The implication was that this is what could happen to local housing departments through the new estate based offices.

1.27   In Britain, Power claimed, additional pressures were at work. Councils were losing political support because of their poor record on the estates. Tenants were forming effective groups to force change. Financial pressure required a reduction in empty, non rent gathering property. Power believed that once an estate office was open it would become a focus for tenant pressure. The very presence of workers and especially an estate manager, was the key. They could identify with the problems on the estate and gain job satisfaction from doing something about them. More significantly, the staff would be accessible to the tenants and find it less easy to escape from their demands. It was part of PEP's function to foster such community action. This would begin to build confidence and increase informal social control. Crime and vandalism would decline. Physical improvements and better management would make the estates more attractive to a wider range of tenants, not just those in desperate need. This would stabilise and then spread the social mix.

1.28   One of the central questions to be examined in this research is whether these countervailing incentives can be great enough to overcome the powerful pressures for social disintegration.

**Other diagnoses**

1.29   There are two distinguishing features of this analysis. One was the multi-causal explanation of housing decline and the importance laid on housing management as the focal point for change.

1.30   Other diagnoses, while not formally espousing single causes for the ghettoisation, poor housing conditions and social malaise, do lay particular stress on factors other than the quality of housing management. We review some of these below.

*(i) Architectural determinism*

1.31   Critical comments on the social effects of high rise developments can be found from its earliest manifestations (Jephcott 1971). However, two writers have come to encapsulate the view that it was the architectural failures of the sixties, in particular, that created social problems - Oscar Newman (1972) and Alice Coleman (1985). For Newman the essential mistake of the mass public housing architecture of the period was that it ignored the importance of surveillance and private space. Householders had a sense of responsibility for their own gardens or back yards or the visible street outside their house. Public areas, especially hidden ones, became the targets for vandalism and the site of crime. Remedies, therefore, lay in adapting the physical structures, providing surveillance, introducing private space, giving people front or back yards or entry phones to blocks. Coleman extends her criticism from architectural design to "Utopian" planning in general, including the low density new towns in the same category as the high rise blocks. The core of her empirical work nevertheless concentrates on the design features of the high density blocks in London. She used measures of physical abuse of the property as a kind of proxy for social malaise - the extent of litter, graffiti, damage to property, urine, faeces and, in a different dimension, numbers of children in care. She found these measures to be strongly correlated with the number of dwellings served by a common entrance, the number of dwellings per block, the number of storeys per block, overhead walkways and other design features. Her remedies are therefore structural - remove overhead walkways, increase the "autonomy" of individual blocks by getting rid of "confused space", reduce anonymity and improve entrances and the general "streetscape".

1.32   It would be wrong to suggest that design and physical improvements are not part of the PEP approach. They are. Moreover, the principle of seeking to recreate private space has been influential in the kind of designs PEP has supported. The difference lies in the importance it is given and the lasting effect it is predicted to have on its own.

1.33   PEP believe that design change is, in many cases, not necessary. Intensive caretaking and recreating tenant pride can achieve as much. Moreover, the effect of design change will only be short lived without good management. Entry phones will quickly become vandalised, for example. Unpopular designs do have an effect but they do so by affecting the social mix on the estate as much as by any direct causal link. Above all there is relatively little that can be done about the design features on many estates without spending sums that are unlikely to be available.

1.34   Newman's and Coleman's views did not go unchallenged by architects either, of course (Hillier 1973, 1986). There are contested views about whether it is the private nature of space that matters or its potential surveillance. Common courtyards may be regularly overlooked and social control exerted that way, for example (Hillier and Hanson 1984; Teymore et al 1988). PEP's approach to design was eclectic. It was seen as useful to help turn the tide of tenant involvement and restore pride in the estate.

*(ii)   Residualisation*

1.35   A different literature gives primacy to social and economic changes and to housing policies that have reduced the scale of council housing, leaving it primarily for the very poorest and those without jobs. This group grew to comprise about two thirds of all public housing tenants by 1990. Residualisation is defined by Malpass and Murie (1982) as "a process whereby public housing moves towards a position in which it provides only a safety net for those who for reasons of poverty, age or infirmity cannot obtain suitable accommodation in the private sector." (p174) Some writers give more emphasis to the Government's housing policy (Forrest and Murie 1988), and others to social and economic change. The whole process has gone much further in parts of the United States where public housing has always taken a smaller share of the housing market. The ghettoisation of the very poorest in Chicago's vast high rise blocks, for example, has created a spiral of decline far more serious than anything experienced in the UK. Julius Wilson (1987) describes the extent to which those living in these areas have become members of what is almost another society, and in which links with and role models from the rest of black society have disappeared. Crack gangs become the main source of income and the most evident power on the estates. They became the geographical site of an underclass made more persistent by its very isolation. In his latest work Wilson (1991) gives especial emphasis to the economic changes that have transformed cities like Chicago in the past decade.

*(iii)  Government regulation and monopoly*

1.36   To many economists the cause of the problem is simple (Minford 1987). Government itself, over the years, has created the situation. Rent control has destroyed a private market, a public monopoly in the provision of accommodation for poor people has grown up and all the deficiencies we have previously described are what one would predict from any public monopoly.

Tenants have no chance to exercise their power of exit as they would in a true free market and any attempt to increase their " voice " through estate boards or otherwise is a weak and inadequate substitute to restoring the free market.

**How much can housing management achieve?**

1.37 The importance of these other explanatory models is that they all suggest that powerful forces are at work driving in the opposite direction to the goals of the PEP projects. Neither PEP nor the DoE have ever denied this. The question is how far can an external agent acting on one part of a set of interacting forces achieve change? That is what this research project set out to discover.

# Chapter 2     The research questions and method

2.2 The research was designed to answer three broad questions:

(i) How far is it possible to decentralise local authority housing department functions to an estate level and what are the barriers to that process, if any?

(ii) What impact does such a strategy have on the quality of the housing service provided, on the quality of the physical environment, on tenant involvement in the management process and on the satisfaction of the tenants with the service provided?

(iii) What are the links between a changed housing environment, more active staff presence on the ground, tenant involvement, attitudes to the estate, the extent of informal social controls and crime on the estates?

2.2 This report is primarily concerned with the first two questions. The association of housing management with levels of crime is the subject of a separate report by the Home Office (Hope and Foster 1993).

**Research design**

2.3 The chosen research design was that of a small scale but very intensive social experiment (Rivlin 1971). Only close observation could determine exactly how far all the elements in the decentralised package had been implemented and a lot of careful work would be necessary to extract reliable performance indicators and sensitive measures of the changing environment. Most of all, high quality crime statistics, including a detailed understanding of the dynamics of crime on an estate, required close observation. The sheer cost of such an approach kept down the number of estates that could be studied at one time. In the end it was decided to choose two "experimental" estates on which PEP was about to begin work and two "control" estates nearby of a similar character, with similar problems but on which no changes were proposed. Two estates were in London and two were in the north of England. (The estates are described more fully in Chapter Four). The projects were scheduled to begin in mid 1987 and the field work lasted from June 1987 to June 1990. There were five elements to the overall research design.

1. A detailed survey of tenants that took the form of a lengthy, largely pre-coded interview schedule. This included questions on the household, its coming to the estate, the views about life on the estate, experience of the housing service and experience of crime. The same survey was administered before the decentralised approach had begun in June 1987 and three years later in June 1990.

2. The collection of statistical information on the performance of the separate elements in the local authorities' landlord function - lettings, repair and maintenance of the property and collection of the rent. This involved extracting material from the authorities' records and in some cases from the original repairs dockets and similar primary sources.

3. An environmental survey of the quality of life -measures of the extent of rubbish, damage to property, graffiti and litter. Quantitative scales were supported by regular photographic surveys.

4. Regular semi-structured interviews with estate officers, other local officials and others with experience of the areas.

5. An ethnographic study which provided detailed knowledge about relationships between tenants, the various subcultures and crime.

Each of these approaches is described in more detail in the appendix.

2.4 This report deals with the housing components of the research which was funded by the DoE, not with the crime aspects which are the subject of the Home Office report (Hope and Foster 1993).

**The limits to experimental research in the social sphere**

2.5 Experimental design has been a powerful means of extending scientific and medical knowledge. It has not been widely used in social research for several very good reasons. It is difficult to draw a completely random sample of experimental and control subjects; those who are the subject of the experiment are likely to know and to be affected by that knowledge. The world of social policy never stands still nor can the control areas be put in quarantine or kept in laboratory conditions. All these factors came into play in this experiment to some extent, as we predicted they would, and it is important to be clear about them at the outset.

**How representative?**

2.6 The experimental estates were taken from a batch that were being considered for inclusion in the Estate Action Programme by the DoE and PEP in 1986. None were as deprived as some of the very worst estates, tackled in the early years of PEP. But they were similar to many others with which PEP was then working. The control estates proved well matched in most respects (see Chapter 4).

**True controls?**

2.7 Early in the literature on social experiments one commentator pointed to a paradox that afflicted experiments in social policy (Timpane 1972). If an idea was a good one, or at least appealing, it would get widespread acceptance before the research results were in. Experimental new ideas had a contagious effect that was likely to "infect" the "control" sites. Precisely this happened in our research, in particular on one control estate. The general idea of decentralisation in housing departments gained considerable ground during the course of the research. However, there are many forms of decentralisation and that undertaken on one of the control estates was rather different in character, providing an opportunity for comparison. This enriched rather than undermined the research design.

2.8 Another kind of problem has been less discussed. What happens if the full "treatment" is not applied? There may be local resistance to implementing the proposals. PEP is, after all, an independent organisation and local authorities are under no obligation to follow its precepts to the full. This happened in this experiment. We describe later what elements were implemented to what degree.

**The model to be tested**

2.9 The overall research design was intended to test a predicted model of interaction between housing service standards, other social variables and crime. The reasoning can be summarised as follows.

2.10 Analysis of crime rates on a small area basis showed a remarkable concentration of crime on poor housing estates (Hope and Hough 1988). Criminological theories suggest there might be a strong link between neighbourhood conditions, informal social controls and crime. The housing service could potentially contribute to reducing crime in three ways.

1. Good housing management could reduce the levels of property damage, graffiti and general physical damage on an estate. Wilson and Kelling (1982) suggested these "incivilities" in themselves created a climate in which anti-social action was followed by crime. By reducing the extent of such property damage the spiral might be checked.

2. Tenant involvement, encouraged by housing managers, might strengthen the sense of social solidarity and encourage more informal social control.

3. Structural change may make the property less vulnerable to abuse, burglary and assault. The interactions predicted in the housing literature mapped onto these criminological theories and a simplified version of the combined model underlying the research is presented in Figure 2.1.

*Figure 2.1* **The model**

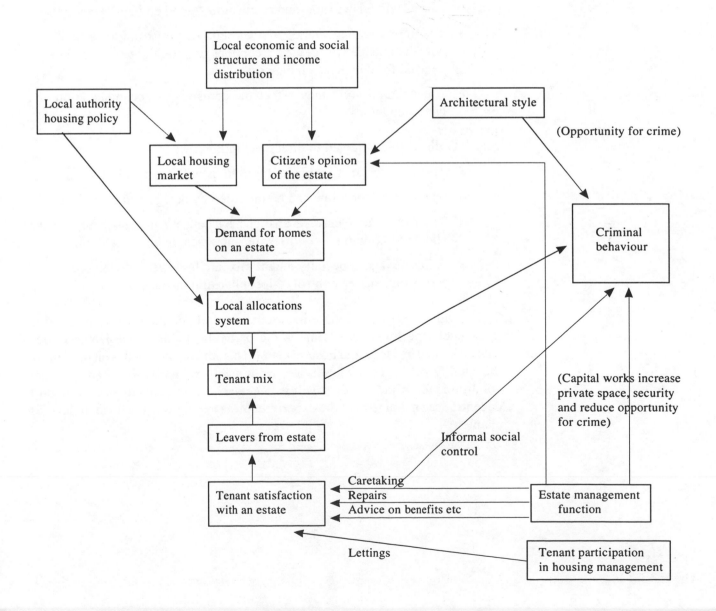

- The local economic and social structure and income distribution affect the local housing market and citizens' perceptions of public housing. The local housing market, shortages or surpluses, and citizens' perceptions of particular estates affect the demand for accommodation on them.

- Local authority policy on house building over many years will have affected the housing market.

- The local authority housing policy with respect to allocations procedure, and the system of priority weightings, will determine the number and type of tenants moving on to the estate and hence the tenant mix. [Tenant mix is predicted to have an impact on levels of criminal behaviour; certain age groups for example are more highly associated with high crime rates.]

- Tenant mix will also be affected by movements off the estate. Tenants' satisfaction with life on the estate may, in part, encourage them to stay but that willingness will also be a function of the housing market and the local authority's wider policies. Nevertheless, the quality of the housing service may act as a change agent in the following way. It may improve the living environment through better oversight and caretaking. This may increase tenant satisfaction and mean that more tenants will wish to stay and retain more "good citizens" among them.

- The improved appearance of the estate may also improve its image with the outside world, the perceptions of potential tenants and hence demand for tenancies on the estate.

- Architectural style may affect the demand for accommodation and hence tenant mix.

2.11 Crime is thus affected in direct and indirect ways.

- The local social structure and traditions will exert an influence.

- Opportunity for crime can be modified by design and capital works.

- The factors that may be changed by housing management, are the slide into growing incivilities, tenant cohesion and tenant mix.

- All these, and especially tenant mix, are however also the product of forces outside the control of local housing managers.

2.12 Only by observing these interactions closely could we hope to develop the model. The impact on crime is the particular focus of the Home Office study reported by Hope and Foster (1992). This study concentrates on measuring the quality of the housing service, its impact on "incivilities" and the pre conditions for crime. To do this it is necessary to define clearly what kind of decentralised management the experiment was testing. That is done in the next chapter.

# Chapter 3

# The PEP prescription

3.1 As we have already observed, PEP has had a distinctive and detailed view about the kind of decentralisation that was appropriate for local housing departments.

3.2 Many local authorities have decentralised their functions to neighbourhood offices. The aim has been to provide a local focus for many of their services and to provide one office to which local residents could go about a range of services from social services to housing, planning and education. This has some advantages but the organisational characteristics of services are very different. Education is organised around schools and colleges, especially since the local management of schools was introduced. For social services the appropriate unit may be the patch team or local residential home.

3.3 For PEP the essential housing unit of management is the estate, or on very large estates, a part of the estate. It is usually a geographically distinct group of dwellings. They are often built at the same time to a common ground plan, sharing design features and problems. It is above all the unit with which residents normally associate. The estate, PEP argue, must therefore be the focus of the intensive management style it advocates.

3.4 On each estate, and for each group of a thousand or so dwellings, there must be an estate office run by a project manager who is responsible for the performance of the landlord function at that level.

*"Each local office will have to put together with the local authority the working system to cover the basic functions of estate management, rents, lettings, repairs, environmental maintenance, and welfare. Estate based management will only work if a number of key elements are carried out within the local organisation."* (Power 1987, p3).

**The 1987 model**

3.5 The PEP Guide to Local Housing Management that was published in 1987 set out a ten item list of essential ingredients.

1. A local estate based office.

2. A local repairs team.

3. Local lettings - a local list of applicants, local procedures for signing on and allocating tenants within an agreed priority scheme.

4. Local control of rent collection and arrears.

5. Resident caretaking, cleaning and open space maintenance with local supervision.

6. Residents' liaison with management - in most cases this will take the form of a residents' forum, in some cases residents may wish to go as far as forming a local cooperative.

7. Capital improvements though small scale in nature.

8. Well-trained but flexible staff given authority to act.

9. The project manager is the key worker held accountable for the outcomes on the estate.

10. An estate budget should show the expenditure allocated to the estate for day to day management and maintenance and be controlled by the project manager.

This was the model tested in this project. The PEP Guide claimed for it that:

*"Estates and their environments are cleaner, thanks mainly to resident caretakers and wardens being part of the local team and in friendly contact with the tenants.*

*Empty dwellings are reduced in all projects where local lettings and local repairs teams operate.*

*Local repairs teams reduce the backlog and increase the speed of repair.*

*Rent arrears can be contained and fall sightly in most projects.*

*Residents become actively involved but do not assume direct management responsibilities.*

*Wider social problems cannot be resolved .. but general services can be dramatically improved.*

*Estate staff find their jobs more rewarding."*

**The PEP method of working**

3.6 Although the estates involved are sometimes referred to as PEP estates, they are not. PEP does not run them, employ the main line staff or carry any direct accountability for them. It does aim to work closely with the local authority concerned but in order to fulfil its brief it assigns consultants to advise the housing department about the form the decentralisation should take and then works with the local staff and tenants. It works at different levels in the authority to achieve a more localised service on the nominated estate and aims to influence the housing service elsewhere in the authority.

3.7 To quote Anne Power, "PEP acts as a catalyst for change, as arbiter between tenants and council, between central and local management, between politicians and officers and tenants, between the DoE and local authorities, facilitating an autonomous local management and maintenance structure at estate level." It works as a broker at the interstices of policy, power and management.

3.8 Though it has its own clear philosophy, it claims not to be dogmatic but to be prepared to support any member of staff who has been attempting to improve local services in ways that clearly worked.

3.9 This arms length relationship with local authorities clearly limits the impact it can make. There is always a danger that local authorities will only implement part of the recommendations or do so in a half hearted way. The people working on a day to day basis are the employees of the local authority. Their careers will depend on seniors in that authority not on PEP and they will be there long after PEP has disappeared from the scene. We shall be exploring these dilemmas as they occurred on the experimental estates.

*Part Two*

IMPLEMENTING DECENTRALISATION

# Chapter 4

# The estates and the local context

4.1   The work of any local housing agency is largely affected by the nature of the local economy and housing market, the social history of the area and the nature of the housing stock. The estates chosen for this study were in contrasting parts of Britain. One pair were in the East End of London. The other pair were in Hull, once a relatively prosperous northern city, more recently suffering from high unemployment as its traditional industries collapsed. To understand the problems the housing departments and the tenants faced it is necessary to paint a brief sketch of the two areas and the social history of the estates.

**Tower Hamlets**

4.2   Tower Hamlets has a history of housing immigrants from the French Huguenots to the Irish, Jewish and Chinese newcomers in the 19th century to the Bengalis and Asians in recent years. Originally proximity to the docks explained the attraction. Today it is the existence of cheap, unpopular and hence available housing.

4.3   The extent of poverty in the area in the late nineteenth century attracted the attention of Charles Booth, Dr.Barnado and University settlements like Oxford House and Toynbee Hall.

4.4   In 1900 the population had reached 1 million, but by the Second World War it had declined to 450,000 and it continued to drop until 1984 when the population had fallen to about 150,000. In 1964 Tower Hamlets was created from an amalgamation of Poplar, Stepney and Bethnal Green Metropolitan Borough councils.

4.5   In the nineteenth century much poor quality housing was built. Slum clearance began in the 1930's but it was the blitz that cleared large areas and made many houses unsafe. The replacement of this property with local authority housing on a large scale began after the Second World War, gathered momentum through the sixties and seventies until halted by the economic crisis of the 1970s. The GLC had undertaken much of this work because it had access to greater resources than the poor councils of the East End. In 1985, when the GLC handed over its housing to Tower Hamlets, it had 30,000 properties in comparison with the 18,000 owned by Tower Hamlets. Tower Hamlets thus became the owner of 80% of all housing in the Borough.

4.6   Unusually for a London borough, Tower Hamlets had a rising population in the 1980s. The increase had two causes. One was the conversion of riverside commercial property into housing and the development of housing in Docklands, bringing an influx of 30-44 year old higher income households. The other was the increasing birthrate which followed the arrival of wives from the New Commonwealth to join husbands who were already here. Projections in 1990 saw the Bengali population rising from 23,000 in 1986 to 35,000 in 1991 and 60,000 in 2001. The problems faced were not like those of the earliest PEP projects. The estates were not hard to let in the way many of those had been. The changing cultural mix and the poverty of the areas were what distinguished them.

4.7 In 1987 nearly three quarters of the tenants were UK born white British households. Three years later the proportion had fallen to two thirds (see Table 4.1). On the control estate over a quarter of the tenants were from Bangladesh both in 1987 and 1990.

*Table 4.1* **Ethnic group of tenants on London estates (%)**

| | Experimental | | Control | |
|---|---|---|---|---|
| | 1987 | 1990 | 1987 | 1990 |
| Bangladeshi | 6 | 8 | 27 | 28 |
| Indian | - | 1 | - | - |
| Pakistani | 1 | - | 2 | 2 |
| East African | - | - | - | - |
| Chinese | 8 | 2 | - | - |
| Vietnamese | 1 | 1 | - | - |
| Caribbean/West Indian | 1 | 7 | 2 | 3 |
| African | 3 | 1 | 1 | 2 |
| Somali | - | - | - | - |
| Irish | - | - | 3 | - |
| Greek Cypriot | - | - | - | - |
| Turkish Cypriot | - | - | - | - |
| UK/British Asian | 1 | 4 | 1 | 1 |
| UK/British Black | 6 | 4 | 2 | 2 |
| UK/British White | 73 | 66 | 56 | 53 |
| Other | - | 2 | 4 | 6 |
| Not Stated | 1 | - | - | - |
| Base = 100% | 242 | 278 | 382 | 393 |

Source: *Tenant surveys*

4.8 The effects of the population changes can be seen in the school adjoining the experimental estate where, despite the closure of a neighbouring school, the number of pupils had fallen to 97 in 1984. During the period of the study the school had 240 pupils and was turning pupils away for lack of space. In the early eighties it was decided not to put families in the deck access blocks on the experimental estate because they were considered unsuitable for family living. Pressure of demand from larger families forced a change of policy. The four-bedroomed maisonettes in the deck access blocks had to be used for incoming families again.

4.9 In 1981 Tower Hamlets had the worst level of unemployment in London (19%). By 1989 it was still the second worst with 13%. The rate in the ward containing the experimental estate was higher than this: (23% men and 8% women) while in the ward containing the control estate it was lower than the Tower Hamlets average perhaps because of its proximity to the City (12%: men 15%, women 6%).

4.10 While there was work in the rag trade and in the furniture trade, it was often erratic and poorly paid. There were some large firms in the area, the NHS was a big employer and Docklands development produced some local jobs. Again the jobs tended to be low paid. The average number of families on Housing Benefit in Tower Hamlets at the time of our research was over 50%. On the experimental estate it was 54% and on the control estate 48%. Nationally, in England and Wales in 1987 the figure was even higher at 66%.

4.11   The Docklands Housing Needs survey in 1986 found that 47% of Tower Hamlets households had an income of less than £5,200. The ILEA found that out of all the London boroughs, Tower Hamlets had the highest percentage of primary school children on free school meals (69%) and families with no wage earner (44%). However, it had the **lowest** percentage of children in care (0.3%) and the second lowest number of single parent families (19%). These last two figures are attributed to the stability of the family unit in the Bengali community from which a high proportion of children come.

4.12   At its creation in 1964, Tower Hamlets Council was solidly Labour, but Labour's monopoly of power was broken in 1978 by the Liberals who took over one ward, concentrating on "community politics". By 1986 they had gained a majority of seats. Their hold on the Council was further strengthened in 1990. They pursued a programme of decentralisation creating seven neighbourhoods each with its own Chief Executive local councillors and delegated functions. Only two of the seven Neighbourhoods that they had created remained in Labour hands. The two research estates were in these two Neighbourhoods.

4.13   The decentralisation meant great changes for many staff. Not enough suitable staff could be recruited and staff turnover was high. Competent people were quickly promoted from the front line.

**The housing department**

4.14   The housing department in Tower Hamlets was a very new creation when it was decentralised to a neighbourhood basis. Other similar boroughs (cf. Hackney) had created comprehensive housing services in the seventies pulling together all the different parts of the local authority that serviced housing. In Tower Hamlets the Treasurer's department had continued to manage rents while the works department dealt independently with repairs in a pattern familiar in the 1950s and 1960s. It was the transfer of 30,000 properties from the GLC that produced the change. This transfer was supposed to be masterminded by a joint committee but the politicians of the GLC were unable to agree with their more traditional Tower Hamlets counterparts and in the end the two departments planned the transfer separately. The effects of this were still to be seen. The mobile cleaning teams set up by the GLC did not accept Tower Hamlets' changes in their contracts and continued to clean in the same way they had always done with no referral to local caretakers or local manager. Ex-GLC tenants continued to pay rent on a 52 week cycle compared to Tower Hamlets tenants who had a rent holiday at Christmas.

**The estates in Tower Hamlets**

**The experimental estate**

4.15   The experimental estate consisted partly of low rise blocks of flats (three pre-war blocks, six built in the fifties, and three in the early sixties). These were built and managed by Tower Hamlets. There are also two deck access blocks built for the GLC in 1974 using industrialised building techniques and managed by them until 1985. The estate contained a few low rise houses many of which were sold under the Right to Buy arrangements. There were also some dwellings which were "listed buildings" and therefore the range of repairs and replacement options was restricted. One of the thirties blocks was a ten minute walk away from the rest of the "estate". The two principal parts of the estate, the deck access blocks and the rest were divided by a very busy road. So there was no obvious cohesive community or housing administration area. There was a wide range of property types and form of construction. The total number of properties included for the purposes of the research was 467 which was rather smaller than estates on which PEP normally worked.

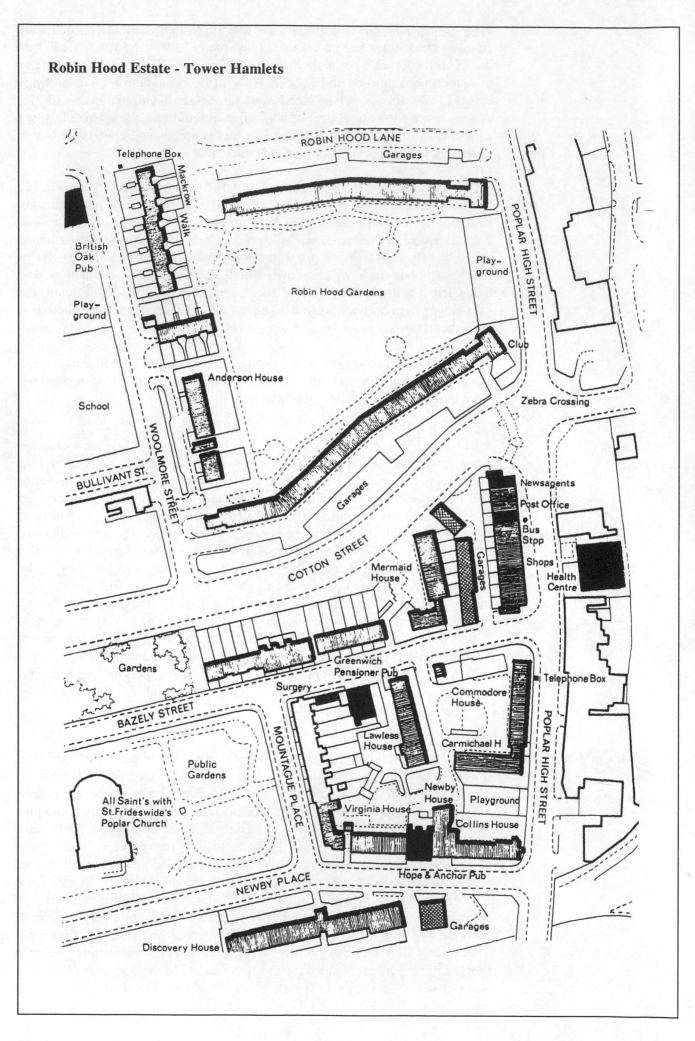

# Robin Hood Estate - Tower Hamlets

ROBIN HOOD LANE

Garages

Telephone Box

Mackrow Walk

British Oak Pub

Play-ground

Robin Hood Gardens

Play-ground

POPLAR HIGH STREET

School

Anderson House

Club

Zebra Crossing

WOOLMORE STREET

BULLIVANT ST.

Garages

Newsagents

Post Office

Bus Stop

Shops

COTTON STREET

Mermaid House

Garages

Health Centre

Gardens

Greenwich Pensioner Pub

Telephone Box

BAZELY STREET

Surgery

Commodore House

MOUNTAGUE PLACE

Lawless House

Carmichael H

Public Gardens

All Saint's with St.Frideswide's Poplar Church

Virginia House

Newby House

Playground

Collins House

POPLAR HIGH STREET

Hope & Anchor Pub

NEWBY PLACE

Garages

Discovery House

The area managed by the estate team was extended during the course of the research.

4.16   The deck access blocks were designed by Alison and Peter Smithson in 1972 as a product of the "social awareness" school of modern architecture. The Smithsons' approach was "behavioural", in the sense that they tried to find a new social form, suited to modern society which retained identity for the individual. Robin Hood Gardens, therefore, incorporated Le Corbusier's idea of "streets in the air". The seven and ten storey blocks were "hinged" to follow the site boundaries. The blocks were designed to serve as walls enclosing a central space intended as a quiet green area to be shared by all the inhabitants and protected from the traffic crowded surrounding streets. The whole project was segregated physically from the traffic by a "moat" in the form of a sunken service road. The approach to the dwellings was to be through the street in the air - a deck for every third floor. The entrances to the units were recessed back from the decks to create "social pockets" and led into kitchens, whilst the living and bedrooms were connected by an internal staircase leading either up or down. The quieter spaces of bedrooms and kitchens were placed so that they faced the central open space, whilst the living rooms and the decks faced the streets around the outside of the blocks. The structure was of load bearing walls and flat slabs with precast concrete panels and mullions. While there was some crumbling ("spalling") of the concrete, the basic structure was sound. The dwellings themselves were spacious and well designed.

4.17   The older part of the estate was of more traditional construction and therefore presented generally well understood repair problems. There was considerable crumbling of the concrete on the older blocks and there was little evidence of regular maintenance. The drains for some of the older blocks were in an appalling condition. The oldest blocks tended to have the worst accommodation, small kitchens and bathrooms, and no lifts.

4.18   The buildings the new GLC blocks replaced were notorious slums and their bulldozed remains were piled in the middle of the central area and covered with grass! Many of the residents of this original community were rehoused on the estate and some remain. For the most part, however, the changes have been considerable.

4.19   Crime on the estate, as reported in the tenant survey prior to the experiment, was only slightly above the average for similarly deprived housing areas in the country as a whole. This was still consistent with tenants' suffering several times the national average levels of crime, however. In the year before the experiment began in 1987, 60 out every 100 tenants had been the victim of some kind of offence that affected their property and seven people suffered personal offences assault, theft from the person or sexual offences.

4.20   Overall, it must be said, this estate was not considered to be at the point of collapse or crisis as was the case for many of the estates on which PEP worked in its early days and was still the case in some other areas. This was an estate representative of many poor and neglected housing areas but not one in free fall. The chance to achieve dramatic results was therefore less. But, by the same token it was a better test of the case for decentralisation in non crisis situations. These comments should not be taken to imply that the estate was looked on favourably by outsiders. It was not and this affected applications to move onto the estate.

**The control estate**

4.21   The control estate also contained a mixture of property types although the estate was generally more modern than the experimental estate. Three tower blocks (1968/70), two modern balcony access blocks with linked walkways (1965 and 1977), a few bungalows and houses (1968) and one walk up, balcony block (1938) made up that part of the control estate that had been run by the GLC. Some of the houses had been sold to their tenants and some of the new owners had made significant changes to the outside elevations of individual dwellings. Separate, but close by, was another estate consisting of three balcony blocks (1954). This part, which had always been managed by Tower Hamlets, was included in the control group of dwellings. When management was decentralised these blocks were managed by a different team from that managing the ex-GLC properties.

4.22   There were serious problems of crumbling concrete in the prewar blocks and on some of the more modern blocks, but like the experimental estate most of the problems were caused by misuse of facilities and vandalism.

4.23   Two of the nineteen thirties blocks were considered the worst possible homes for tenants and were allocated to those in serious arrears. The 1938 block was used to house Bengalis. GLC policy, in practice although not in theory, had been to allocate Bengalis together in the worst property. There was a lot of squatting on the control estate when the research began which was largely eliminated by the end of the research period. This estate was much nearer the City of London than the experimental estate and as the research continued this factor came to have more influence. The houses on the estate were more attractive to single people or younger married couples working in the City or other professional people.

4.24   At the outset in 1987 the social class composition of the two London estates was very similar (see Table 4.2).

*Table 4.2*   **Social group of household: London estates (1987) (%)**

|  | Experimental | Control |
|---|---|---|
| AB Professional and intermediate | 3 | 4 |
| C1 Non-manual skilled | 11 | 15 |
| C2 Manual skilled | 14 | 12 |
| D Partly skilled | 24 | 26 |
| E Unskilled | 47 | 43 |
| Base = 100% | 242 | 382 |

Source: *Tenant Surveys*

4.25   Roughly 70% were in the unskilled or semi skilled categories. In the three years of the research the number of social group E tenants on the control estate fell, to be replaced by category D. The experimental estate's social composition changed little. The number of tenants working full time fell from 29% to 20% on the experimental estate and from 31% to 24% on the control estate (see Table 4.3).

**Hull**

4.26   Hull is a city with a prosperous past. Its huge expansion occurred during the industrial revolution both because of its position on the Humber and Hull rivers, where it was a pivotal point between the sea and internal navigable waterways, and because of the industry that developed in the city itself. The

# St George's Estate - Tower Hamlets

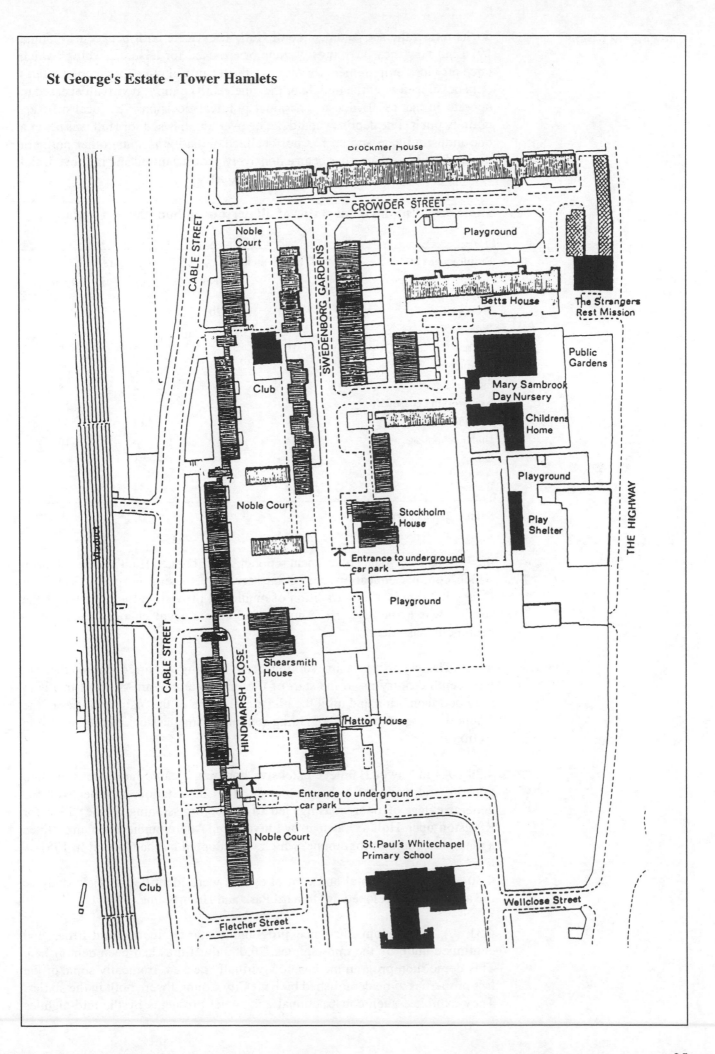

docks reflect the rise and decline of Hull. They were built between 1775 and 1914 but now they have mostly gone or are used for leisure. Fishing (which once provided employment for many of the tenants of our experimental estate) only developed after the middle of the nineteenth century. It virtually ceased to operate in the 1970s due to "national political decisions" as local officials politely put it. The decline should not be over emphasised for Hull was never a one industry place and so has not declined as badly as some other northern towns. The central area has been extensively pedestrianised and improved, and attempts are being made to attract more industry.

*Table 4.3* **Employment status of all persons in household: London estates (%)**

| Employment Status | Experimental | | Control | |
|---|---|---|---|---|
| | 1987 | 1990 | 1987 | 1990 |
| Works FT | 29 | 20 | 31 | 24 |
| Works PT | 5 | 5 | 4 | 3 |
| Retired | 16 | 13 | 15 | 9 |
| FT student | 12 | 24 | 12 | 25 |
| Sick/disabled | 3 | 4 | 2 | 4 |
| Non-working housewife | 15 | 15 | 17 | 17 |
| Seeking work | 14 | 8 | 14 | 7 |
| Under school age | 4 | 9 | 4 | 10 |
| Other | 2 | 1 | 1 | 1 |
| Base = 100% | 519 | 682 | 844 | 1136 |

Source: *Tenant Surveys*

4.27   The 1969 local government reorganisation created Humberside authority which controls education and social services. Housing is run by Hull City Council. There is a long tradition of municipal provision. Even the telephone service was owned by the Council until recent legal changes forced it to become independent.

4.28   The big increase in working class housing occurred during the late nineteenth century up to the start of the First World War. Much of this is in very poor condition and until the mid eighties one of the main priorities of the Council's programme was upgrading and improving the stock through Housing Action Areas.

4.29   As in Tower Hamlets, extensive bombing cleared large areas of slum housing and made many houses unsafe. This devastation, together with the general extent of poor housing, led to the commissioning of the "Plan for Kingston-upon-Hull". Drawn up by Lutyens and Abercrombie, the plan outlined a massive building programme, which was adopted by the Council in 1951.

4.30   The experimental and control estates were identified in their study as the areas later developed as Orchard Park and Bransholme.

4.31   A major slum clearance programme started in the mid-fifties and continued until, by the mid-eighties, 26,000 dwellings had been demolished. This demolition programme has now virtually ceased. Ironically some of the last properties to be demolished by Hull City Council were built in the sixties. They exhibited such constructional and social problems by the mid-eighties that the only option seemed demolition. At the beginning of the research, Hull City Council was managing around 40,000 properties.

4.32   Unemployment in the Hull area at the time of the study was about 15%. Two-thirds of the households on the experimental estate received Housing Benefit, roughly the national average, 60% of households on the control estate did. The area of which the experimental estate is a part has the highest number of children on free school meals in Hull, the highest number of children on the child protection register and on supervision orders, and the highest number of probation service clients.

4.33   Although the Conservatives ran Hull City Council for a brief spell from 1969, that was an exception in what has been a Labour stronghold for many years. In 1990, 57 members of the Council were Labour and three Conservative.

4.34   The Council has been pragmatic in its approach. As the Housing Strategy statement put it: "the Council intends to maximise its resources .... by being flexible and opportunistic". Hull City Council had been willing to talk and work with the private sector. The £17m Victoria Dock scheme was one example.

## The housing department

4.35   The context in which housing was managed in Hull is completely different to that in Tower Hamlets. The stability of the housing department could not be in greater contrast. Staff work within the department for year after year, most having been brought up in Hull.

4.36   Despite the changes from localised offices to a more centralised service in the 1970's and then back to more local decentralisation, the Hull housing department remained stable. Staff are proud of their work and their city in ways not expressed by Tower Hamlets staff.

4.37   The process of change to a PEP style office was therefore different from that in Tower Hamlets. While some procedures had to be invented (for local repairs ordering and monitoring of statistics), most existed in other offices in which some staff, at least, had worked. This had the advantage of smoothing the change but had the drawback that procedures were not questioned. As one officer in Hull put it : "When I tell staff to do something they never answer back". This meant the department functioned well but change was only likely to come from the top.

## The estates in Hull
### The experimental estate

4.38   Building work started on Orchard Park, the site of the experimental estate, in the 1960s. The control estate was built in the 1970s as part of the huge Bransholme development.

4.39   The Orchard Park estate is located on the north western outskirts of Hull and contains about 3,500 dwellings and houses 10,000 people.

4.40   The start of building at Orchard Park coincided with the city's decision to raise its house building quota from 800 to 2,000 dwellings per year. It was believed that this could only be achieved by using mass house building techniques. 1963 also marked the beginning of Wimpey's association with Hull. Orchard Park was Wimpey's first major contract of its kind in the north of England. Thus in many respects Orchard Park was an experimental project. A new form of mass produced, though two storey, construction was employed - "no-fines". This involved the use of pre-cast concrete shells. Though speedy to

27

erect it has ever since suffered from problems of internal damp, cold and condensation. The roofs had no overhanging eaves and the rain penetrated the walls.

4.41   Orchard Park was divided into four "villages". One of these had been taken as the site for a PEP project several years before our research began. The experimental site was a neighbouring "village" on which PEP was also to work. It contained not merely the prefabricated two storey terraces we have described but also tower blocks. Of the 1,083 properties about half were houses - 514. There were seven high rise blocks.

4.42   In addition, a non traditional type of layout was employed. Imported from America this consisted of large open areas of grass with no private gardens. Traffic was segregated and pedestrians were meant to walk on separate paths through the estate. They preferred to walk in the road or across areas not designated as paths by the architects!

4.43   It is the parts of Orchard Park which combined five problematic features where the least settled communities were found. These problems were: no-fines construction which left the houses and flats cold and subject to condensation; expensive to run underfloor electric heating; no front gardens with no subsequent privacy; the Radburn layout which has the backs of one row of houses facing the fronts of another; and the fact that 47% of dwellings on the experimental estate were in high-rise blocks of flats. In these areas of Orchard Park, which include the experimental site, tenant turnover was particularly high, rates of crime were high and there was widespread vandalism and a deteriorating environment.

4.44   The levels of crime at the beginning of the study were far higher than in the London estates. In the year before the first tenant survey was conducted, out of every 100 households 98 had suffered some kind of offence against their property and 9 out of a hundred had suffered personal assault, robbery or sexual offences.

4.45   Orchard Park was built to provide homes for slum clearance families many of whom came from the Hessle Road fishing community. This area had a notorious reputation itself and many prospective tenants from other parts of the city simply did not want to live alongside slum clearance families. Like Damer's Wine Alley (1974), Orchard Park became inextricably linked with, and has never recovered from, the stigma of slum clearance (see also Gill 1977; Armstrong and Wilson 1973). As a CES report (1985) noted:

> *Although slum clearance proved a considerable barrier in terms of letting properties on Orchard Park there were other difficulties which exacerbated this problem. Like many other estates built on the periphery of cities, for example Easterhouse in Glasgow, there was no adequate infrastructure to support the estates' population (cf. Nuttgens 1989). When Orchard Park opened there were only eight shops and a small shopping centre for the whole estate and despite the erection of another small shopping complex on the Thorpes and three pubs in the area, the facilities to this day remain woefully inadequate.*

4.46   Orchard Park therefore began its existence with a number of disabling factors as outsiders and insiders alike saw it: poor design and construction, an undesirable location on the North West periphery of the city and the stigma of slum clearance. Each of these factors influenced the tenant profile of the estate.

# The Orchard Park Estate - Hull

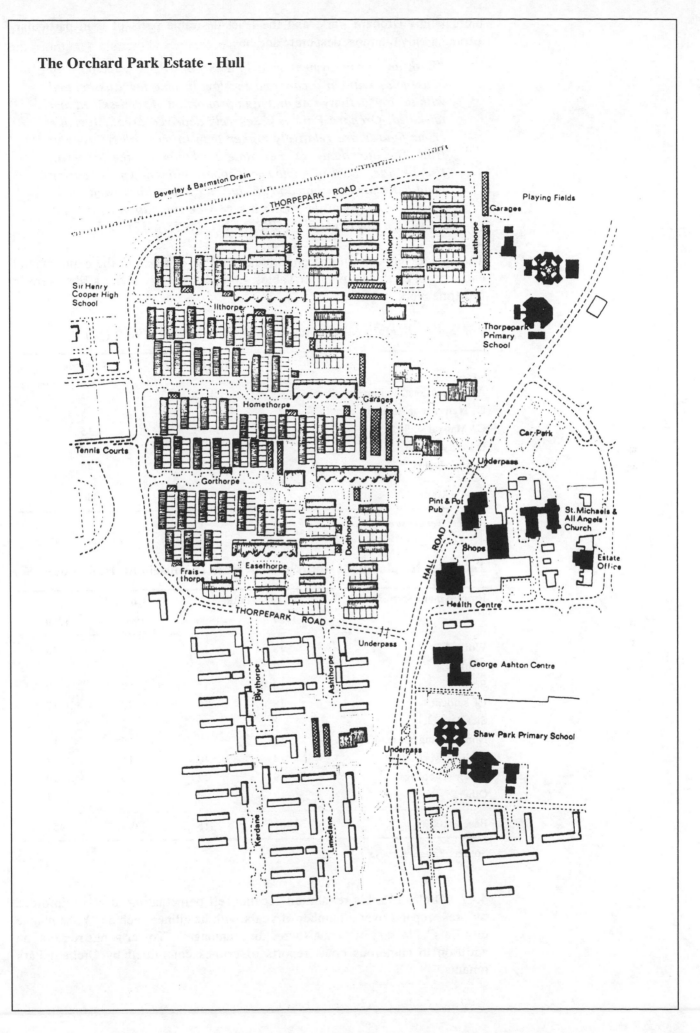

Increasingly Orchard Park, and the least desirable parts of it in particular, attracted only the most desperate and needy.

> *"With an unemployment rate in 1981 of 18.3% with 65% of households without a car, and the low income level associated with the low activity rate and high proportion of semi-skilled and unskilled, Orchard Park is a severely deprived area... Juvenile crime figures are relatively higher than in most other areas of Hull. The attendance at the estate's schools are the lowest in Humberside... Lack of employment opportunities and poor housing conditions have combined to produce a cycle of blight and social malaise, and given the estate a city-wide reputation as a "sink estate", in low demand." (CES Report, 1985:16/17).*

The social composition and employment status of those in the experimental and control estates is given in Tables 4.4 and 4.5. Only about a fifth were in full time work.

*Table 4.4*  **Social group of household: Hull estates (1987) (%)**

|  | Experimental | Control |
|---|---|---|
| AB Professional and intermediate | 1 | 1 |
| C1 Non-manual skilled | 6 | 5 |
| C2 Manual skilled | 15 | 15 |
| D Partly skilled | 26 | 30 |
| E Unskilled | 53 | 49 |
| Base = 100% | 578 | 480 |

Source: *Tenant surveys*

*Table 4.5*  **Employment status of all persons in household: Hull estates (%)**

| Employment Status | Experimental | | Control | |
|---|---|---|---|---|
|  | 1987 | 1990 | 1987 | 1990 |
| Works FT | 18 | 19 | 22 | 23 |
| Works PT | 7 | 5 | 8 | 8 |
| Retired | 12 | 11 | 9 | 9 |
| FT student | 18 | 19 | 20 | 17 |
| Sick/Disabled | 3 | 3 | 2 | 2 |
| Non-working housewife | 18 | 17 | 16 | 15 |
| Seeking work | 14 | 10 | 11 | 8 |
| Under school age | 9 | 12 | 9 | 10 |
| Other | 2 | 4 | 3 | 7 |
| Base = 100% | 1407 | 1415 | 1396 | 1455 |

Source: *Tenant surveys*

4.47   Orchard Park's reputation became self perpetuating. It was reinforced by press reports over a number of years with headlines such as "Yobs plague city flats", "Misery of vandals wrecking rampage", "Tower gangs run riot" in addition to numerous court reports of crimes committed by Orchard Park tenants.

4.48   Behind the sensational headlines, the majority of law abiding tenants resent outsiders' condemnation of the place that has been their home, in many cases since the estate was first opened.

**The control estate**

4.49   The control estate was more socially settled than the experimental site. There were more front gardens and though 30% of the dwellings were in flats they were contained within rows of houses with four flats sharing a communal entrance. These features and the proximity to better shopping facilities probably explain why the right to buy sales were higher and tenant turnover lower on the control estate.

4.50   Nevertheless, the estates both had similarly small numbers of social groups A,B and Ci. The control estate had a slightly smaller number of groups E and more group D but the social composition at the start of the research was not very different from the experimental estate. Nor were the kinds of complaints that tenants made of their homes. Again about two fifths complained of condensation and dampness and a quarter of draughts. Internal and external decorations were felt to be more of a problem on the experimental estate as was rubbish collection (see Table 4.6).

**The London and Hull estates compared**

4.51   The estates did not conform to the stereotypes found in the popular press or indeed more widely. The London inner city tower block estates with mixed ethnic communities did not have the highest crime rates or poverty and unemployment. These were worse in the largely white working class northern estates. The estates were more popular with tenants and had more community spirit than outsiders could conceive. Nevertheless, they were certainly deprived and their inhabitants suffered from crime and neglect on a scale probably unimagined by middle class suburban dwellers.

**Table 4.6   Percentages of respondents for each estate that said item was a 'big problem' in their flat/house in 1987**

|  | Hull | | London | |
|---|---|---|---|---|
|  | Experimental | Control | Experimental | Control |
| Hot water | 3 | 4 | 10 | 11 |
| Keeping your home warm | 22 | 37 | 39 | 42 |
| Condensation and dampness | 39 | 41 | 33 | 35 |
| Draughts | 29 | 25 | 39 | 44 |
| External decorations | 21 | 16 | 32 | 18 |
| Internal decorations | 9 | 6 | 23 | 16 |
| Getting rid of household rubbish | 17 | 9 | 9 | 8 |
| Worn out fixtures and fittings | 22 | 25 | 27 | 21 |
| Worn out switches and light fittings | 10 | 8 | 16 | 8 |
| Upkeep of garden | 7 | 9 | 5 | 1 |
| Base No | 578 | 480 | 242 | 382 |

4.52   The tenant survey showed that nearly two fifths of the tenants in both the London and Hull experimental estates said they were very or fairly dissatisfied with their estate. Again the figure was higher in Hull than in London - 43% compared to 36% but both were disturbing figures. There was plenty to do.

**The Garths Estate - Hull**

Playing Fields

Leeming Garth

Manston Garth

BIGGIN AVENUE

Biggin Av.

Biggin Av.

Biggin Av.

Yeadon Garth

Neatshead G

NODDLE HILL WAY

Primary

Wickenby G

Oakington Garth

Junior

Biggin Hill School

Castle Hill Road

WAWNE ROAD

Playground

Topcliffe Garth

Patrington Garth

Upavon Garth

Scampton Garth

Rufforth G

Fire Station

NODDLE HILL WAY

Playground

# Chapter 5

# Implementing estate based management

5.1 PEP's objectives on the experimental estates were fourfold:

1. to decentralise a number of core housing management functions to an estate level;

2. to give joint control over all these functions to one local manager;

3. to extend the role of the manager to include a wider responsibility for activities on the estate;

4. to make the manager accountable to tenants.

5.2 We discuss the outcome of decentralising each of the core management functions in Part III, and the role of tenants in Chapter Six. Here we give an overview of the process of decentralisation and the difficulties that were encountered. We consider how the practice of management contrasted with the ideal on the experimental estates and to a lesser extent on the control estates. We look at PEP's arguments for estate based housing offices and consider them in the light of this experience.

**Tower Hamlets experimental office**

5.3 In July 1987 when the research began, the local housing management team for the Tower Hamlet's experimental estate had been in post for six months. They had received PEP team training and were working from an old Town Hall, a ten to fifteen minute walk from the furthest part of the estate. The Team Leader did not want to move from the Town Hall until suitable office accommodation could be found. Tenants had resisted the move to takeover the unused community hall for the housing office. The PEP consultant identified a ground floor flat on the estate that could be used for an office. Adaptation work was quickly undertaken and the team opened the office in August 1987.

5.4 The flat was in an older block standing between the two ex-GLC deck access blocks. Plans were drawn up for a new office building more centrally placed with the hope that the London Docklands Development Corporation would provide funding. It became clear during the research period that this would not happen. The area of responsibility covered by the team was expanded in September 1988. The additional part of the estate was even further from the estate office and a further move was planned but not in the period covered by this research.

5.5 Originally the team administered an area containing 434 properties, excluding a few houses purchased by tenants. In September 1987 a further area was added bringing the total to 479. In September 1988 another estate was added making 755, excluding right to buy properties.

5.6 At the beginning one team leader, one estate officer and one administrator were to manage the 434 properties with help from a student on placement. When the number of properties increased to 755 in September 1988, the number of estate officers increased to three plus a student on placement. When one estate officer left, the student was appointed to the post and was not replaced. A housing benefit officer was temporarily placed in the office in 1989 for a trial period of six months. A temporary tenants' liaison officer was appointed for three months in January 1990 to help with capital works consultations with tenants. An administrative trainee also worked in the office.

5.7   The office was always crowded. There was no private interview room, no rest area for staff. The decoration and furnishing of the office was improved in 1988. The office was cramped but not shabby.

5.8   The local repairs team was initially based on the estate, though not in close proximity to the office. In 1989 they moved to a flat nearer the housing office. However, they were not completely locally based, working for the neighbourhood when the direct labour organisation found it necessary. Caretakers reported to the local manager.

## Tower Hamlets control office

5.9   At the start of the research period in July 1987 the large neighbourhood containing the control estate was divided for housing management purposes. In April 1988 the neighbourhood was divided into five areas and a local team was appointed for each. The number of staff was based on PEP guidelines of 350 properties per estate officer. Thus, early on, it moved to resemble the experimental site in some important respects.

5.10   Some of the five area teams were based on estates. The main part of the control estate, however, was administered by a team working from within the neighbourhood housing management building. The main reason given for this was that there was no appropriate building to house the team on the estate. A small part of the control estate, responsibility for which was transferred to a different team, was administered from a shop in a shopping centre in the area. It was a good fifteen minutes walk from the part of the control estate it managed. Thus, the control office, though decentralised, was not properly estate based.

5.11   The main area of the control estate (517 properties) was administered by a team with responsibility for 1200 properties. The smaller part (124 properties) was administered by another team managing 1100 (less right to buy) properties but this office became too busy and a part of the estate was moved to the control of another office. The team administering the 1200 properties was made up of one Area coordinator (team leader), three estate officers, one technical officer (repairs inspections, capital works liaison etc), two housing support workers (administrative and repairs reporting). The team leader managed temporarily to obtain the services of another administrator because of the level of work.

5.12   The team worked from an upstairs office which, while not particularly pleasant, was fairly large. The tenants' reception area downstairs was cramped and unappealing. The smaller part of the control estate was administered from a crowded office. The reception area was most unpleasant with a small, shabby room, a very high reception desk like a barricade and no seats. The repairs team was based on another estate.

5.13   In short, the control estate in London had become decentralised too, early on in the experiment, but it was not decentralised to an estate base nor were the principles of organisation or tenant access those that PEP had espoused. However, it was well run and far from a pure centralised model with which we had intended to contrast the local office on the experimental estate.

**Hull experimental estate**

5.14   The team leader was appointed for the experimental estate in February 1988 and initially he worked from the established PEP office on the neighbouring "village".   The rest of the staff were then appointed and in May 1988 PEP training took place for the staff, the already resident caretakers and the repairs team foreman.   The local repairs team for the two PEP estates started work in April 1988 and repairs could be phoned in to the established PEP office from either estate.   The estate office on the experimental site opened in September 1988 in well converted bicycle sheds at the base of the three grouped tower blocks which formed a focal point for the estate.   Because many tenants passed it on their way to the shops or to catch the bus, the office was well situated.

5.15   The team was to administer 1,083 properties, excluding a few properties bought by the tenants.

5.16   The housing management staff consisted of

1. One Team Leader

2. Two Neighbourhood Housing Assistants (rent arrears/tenant management etc.)

3. Two Reception/Advice/Secretarial/Administrative/Repairs Reporting staff

4. Four caretakers who covered the 7 blocks on the estate and 1 handyman who attempted to keep the unadopted roads and open spaces free of litter besides doing other small jobs round the estate.

5.17   When some extra properties were taken on, the experimental estate and the neighbouring PEP estate were given an extra advice/reception worker and because of the greater pressures in the experimental office, this staff member became wholly based in the experimental estate office.   Each PEP office was given a half-time Neighbourhood Housing Assistant.   A Housing Benefit adviser came into the office on one afternoon a week from April 1990.

5.18   The office was well planned.   There was a spacious central open plan working area, a small office at the back which was taken over by the manager, an interview room and a meeting room which doubled as an extra interview room, staff rest area, and room for quiet working.

5.19   Adjacent to the office was a Portakabin which originally housed the architects and the team managing the environmental improvements.   The architects were pulled back to the centre in 1989.

5.20   The DLO repairs team had offices adjacent to the housing management office (in the base of the tower blocks).   The private contractor team took over these plus an office in the Portakabin.   In short, the Hull experimental office conformed as closely as one might reasonably expect to the PEP model.

**The Hull control office**

5.21   In July 1987 the control estate in Hull was run from an Area office which managed roughly 9,000 properties from an office attached to a large well-maintained, shopping centre.   From October 1989 this office piloted a decentralisation plan for the whole of Hull that involved putting an assistant director into the Area office. The Area was subdivided into three with two management teams run from sub offices and one team continuing to be run from the central office.   Most of the control estate continued to be managed from the central office but a small part was hived off to a sub-office.   While tenants on the control estate had a ten to fifteen minute walk to the Area office it was beside the shopping centre that they were likely to use.

5.22   The control estate was administered by Housing Management Assistants who dealt mainly with arrears and about 800 properties each.   This was reduced to under 500 because it was regarded as a difficult area.   Unlike the experimental estate staff, these HMAs did not do allocations or show new tenants around property.

5.23   The staff worked upstairs in a large open plan office which was enlarged when services were decentralised.  Downstairs the reception area was improved but the improvements were not major.  Tenants had nowhere to sit although there could be a lot of waiting in this busy office.

5.24   Repairs only began to be dealt with from this office in October 1989. They had been run from a DLO depot based in the Area but without links to the housing management office.  From April 1990 some of the repairs service was recentralised.

5.25   Once again then, as in London, the general move to decentralisation came to the control estate  during the research period, reducing the contrast the research had hoped to make between centralised and decentralised working. However, as in London, the form of decentralisation did not conform closely to many of the patterns PEP espoused.  It did give us the opportunity to monitor the consequences of this change and to compare the two.

**A comprehensive service?**

5.26   Tables 5.1 and 5.2 compare the elements of the ideal PEP model with the kind of decentralisation operating in the two research sites.

*Table 5.1*   **The extent and nature of decentralisation in Tower Hamlets (June 1990)**

| Elements in the PEP model | Tower Hamlets experimental | Tower Hamlets control |
|---|---|---|
| 1.   An estate based office | Operational | Localised but not estate based |
| 2.   Local repairs team | Localised for some repairs | Localised for some repairs |
| 3.   Local allocations | Neighbourhood not estate based | As experimental |
| 4.   Local control of rent and arrears | Centralised collection | As experimental |
|  | Neighbourhood level arrears control | As experimental until April 1990 |
| 5.   Estate based caretakers/ cleaners responsible to team leader | Yes | Yes |
| 6.   Tenants actively involved | Some progress | Success in consultation not day to day management |
|  | Particular success with ethnic minority |  |
| 7.   Capital programme | Delays | Substantial |
| 8.   Staffing | Up to recommended levels | As experimental |
| 9.   Project manager | In place | As experimental |
| 10. Estate budget | Some elements begun | Begun |

*Table 5.2*  **The extent and nature of decentralisation in Hull (June 1990)**

| Elements in the PEP model | Hull experimental | Hull control |
|---|---|---|
| 1. An estate based office | Operational | Localised but not estate based |
| 2. Local repairs team | Localised for all repairs | No localised team |
| 3. Local allocations | Yes | Yes |
| 4. Local control of rent and arrears | Area level collection | As experimental |
| | Estate based arrears control | Sub-area based arrears control |
| 5. Estate based caretakers/ cleaners responsible to team leader | Yes (centrally controlled cleaners) | No (no blocks of flats) |
| 6. Tenants actively involved | Good progress with elected sub-committee of housing committee | No progress |
| 7. Capital programme | Large, successful programme. | Small, successful programme |
| | Environmental works progressing slowly | |
| 8. Staffing | Up to PEP recommended levels but under pressure because of workload | Up to PEP levels |
| 9. Project manager | In place | As experimental |
| 10. Estate budget | Begun | Begun |

**Tensions in implementing decentralisation**

5.27 Estate based management runs counter to traditional local authority patterns of standardisation, central routines and practices and close control by councillors. Tensions were, therefore, almost inevitable.

5.28 Councillors and some officials feared that making an estate a local cost centre would help to prepare it for takeover if tenants or anyone else wanted to attempt this. Councillors argued that targeting some estates and involving tenants in management would lead to some estates being treated more favourably than others. They had an overview of the whole borough's housing needs and one group of tenants should not be allowed to step outside that policy.

5.29 The new approach posed problems for central managers:

- How should the centre manage a dispersed group of estates?

- How much control should the centre exercise?

- What was the appropriate way to relate to a local estate office and its staff? * In the PEP model the ability of the team leader becomes crucial. This will become evident in the results of the research in Part III. Yet old local authority structures did not have the capacity to monitor the performance of such individuals effectively.

- A much greater degree of responsibility is demanded of managers in decentralised offices than in centralised systems. This requires personal capacity and training. One new manger was surprised, and initially somewhat overwhelmed, by the level of demands made.

5.30    Attitudes to such greater independence expressed in interviews were ambivalent. Local managers relished the independence to do as they thought best and would describe how they took decisions on issues that previously would have gone to a central manager. On the other hand they often wanted support of some kind and felt that the central managers tended to talk to them only to criticise not to congratulate them. Central managers wanted the local managers to manage and complained that they would not take necessary tough decisions.

5.31    In the Isle of Dogs in Tower Hamlets, the central managers talked of regular meetings with their individual team leaders to discuss particular issues in offices but even when a new programme of meetings was set up these always seemed to peter out quite quickly. There were more pressing problems for the Neighbourhood Managers, e.g. capital works. Day to day humdrum management was left to team leaders until there was a crisis. There were fortnightly meetings with team leaders but these did not offer individual support.

5.32    In Hull the estate based housing manager worked with much the same staff structure and procedures for arrears and allocations as the rest of Hull. So he was implementing a local office with a system set up for centralised work. He had no clear line manager. The PEP coordinator did not fulfil that role and above there was the assistant director, who did not deal with day to day problems on the estates. If anyone took a supportive role it was the PEP consultant. The lack of line management offered the housing manager a lot of freedom but, as he was finding, the problems of the estate were overwhelming.

5.33    The lack of line management also isolated the estate from the wider Hull housing department and meant information on the PEP local estates was not easily passed around Hull despite the imminent decentralisation plan.

5.34    In the localisation in April 1990 the two PEP estates were brought under the line management of an assistant director based in the Area office.

**Estate budgets**

5.35    Both the Tower Hamlets estates had been given similar, if limited, budgets with power to "vire" or switch between headings. By 1990 the budget covered repairs of all kinds, maintenance and grounds. The firmness of these budgets was open to question. A local councillor said she was happy if they overspent because it proved the need for more money for the neighbourhood. However, neighbourhood managers did not take this line. They rapped the experimental estate manager over the knuckles for her first year overspending which she saw as an achievement given that when she started six months into the financial year there was a significant underspend by the team. She was annoyed about the criticism, pointing out the underspend by other team leaders. By contrast on the control estate the team was encouraged to spend a further 70% on top of its agreed 1989/9 budget because of underspend elsewhere in the Neighbourhood.

5.36    In Hull, the experimental estate had more local control of its budget than the control estate even after decentralisation. The budget again primarily covered expenditure on repairs and cleaning. But there was more freedom. A skip could be ordered directly by the team on the experimental estate but on the control estate it had to go through the central finance section. The centre would not give up the control it exercised. A computer programme was written which would allow local spending but give clear central oversight of budgets. The local offices had local budgets but they were not left free to spend them entirely as they saw fit.

**Monitoring of performance**

5.37 PEP argued that strict monitoring of performance (e.g. levels of rent arrears, numbers of voids etc.) should be used as a management tool. We did not observe this happening on the study estates. Statistics were collected partly because of the research, but this work tended to be resented. The figures were handed over to central managers who also did not appear to use them as a management tool but for reports on over all performance of the whole department to councillors on the relevant committees.

5.38 This is not to say that the local office statistics were never used but that they were not taken very seriously nor used on a regular basis. Members of staff were not encouraged to use them to review their own performance. Managers tended to feel that they offered only a partial picture, which was true. But because so much housing management is fairly humdrum and routine, and there is no monetary feedback on how the team is doing, without statistics on performance it is difficult for the team to feel that they are achieving anything or even to identify something to achieve.

**A wider managerial role**

5.39 PEP supported not only more local autonomy but also a wider brief for the local manager. The whole life of the estate was to be considered as part of housing management's efforts to make the estate more attractive. This meant that the manager should be instrumental in increasing job opportunities or training, or improving policing and other such initiatives. Team leaders do not necessarily do the work themselves so much as initiate, coordinate other to do it and work with people who are taking action locally.

5.40 The second team leader on the Tower Hamlets experimental estate took on this wide brief with relish. The estate officer who was acting team leader had applied to the DoE for a grant to create a training centre in a disused laundry. This was inspired by the understanding that training was in favour at the DoE, and that there was some underspend available which needed to be applied for quickly. The new team leader took up the challenge and worked to pull together the resources needed to furnish and equip the centre and to get teachers.

5.41 In Hull, the team leader was more overwhelmed by the housing work, but he called meetings involving other agencies - the police and local head teachers to talk about continuing problems with children, and he took other initiatives such as involving two underemployed Manpower Services Commission scheme workers in a survey of pensioners. On the Hull control estate these extra activities were not in any way regarded as the work of the professional housing manager. We discuss the importance of this wider role later.

## Chapter 6

# The local office

6.1 An estate based office is central to PEP thinking. We consider in this chapter how the experimental estate based offices worked out in practice and how they were different from the decentralised offices on the control estates.

**Accessibility**

6.2 This is affected by the siting of the office, the opening hours and the lay out of the office. The intention is that an estate based housing office put services within easy reach of all tenants. This was true on both our experimental estates. However, good accessibility can be achieved if the office is in an frequented shopping centre as was one of the control offices in Tower Hamlets and the control office in Hull. These shopping centre based offices were heavily used.

6.3 The Hull experimental estate office was open to the public from 9.00am to 12.30 and then from 1.30 to 4.00pm every day. The Tower Hamlets experimental office hours were more restricted, opening from 10.00am to 12.00am and then from 2.00 to 4.00pm (but only four out of five afternoons).

6.4 The total number of tenant callers at the Hull office per day grew from 26 in October 1988 to an average of 45 in April and June 1990 on the sample days observed. In addition other callers from other services and workmen brought the total daily callers to about 100 in 1990, up from 50 in 1988. Telephone calls varied from thirty to fifty a day at the end of the research period, up from twenty a day at the outset.

6.5 Activity levels in London were less. Total callers were between fifty and sixty a day at the end. Telephone calls were greater at nearly fifty a day.

6.6 The informal atmosphere and the ease with which tenants could gain access to staff was clearly greater in both experimental offices compared to the controls and other housing offices.

6.7 Tenant accessibility was not the only outcome. One councillor said it was much easier to penetrate the bureaucracy of the small office than the large ones (which accounts perhaps for some staff opposition to decentralisation). Social services staff in Hull commented on how much easier it was to see housing staff in the experimental office than in the Area office.

6.8 In a small office it is less easy for staff to use a receptionist as a barrier to avoid seeing difficult tenants because staff are right there. Particularly in Hull with the open plan reception area, the build up of them/us antagonism was prevented. On the other hand it was hard to discuss tenants with other staff because other tenants were present in the waiting area. There was a much more positive attitude from staff towards tenants in the Hull experimental office than in some of the Area offices.

6.9 A manager commented that quick action often defuses the kind of situation that builds up in offices with less direct communication between tenants and staff. In a centralised office with a separate reception area, a receptionist will often bear the brunt of tenants' anger.

6.10   However, staff paid a price for this continual availability. It was difficult for them to get on with work when they were summoned whenever a tenant chose to drop in. While staff in the Tower Hamlets experimental estate planned a rota for work on the desk it was difficult to stick to it when they could be seen by the tenant who felt aggrieved because staff were not immediately available. Tenants could and did harass staff over, for instance, repairs that had not been done. Staff had often gone out of their way to persuade a member of the repairs team to go out yet they were blamed because that repairman had not gone. A particular problem in Tower Hamlets was tenants who made repeated visits to the office ostensibly with a request for help but basically for social reasons. One member of the Tower Hamlets staff felt that being estate based made housing staff too available and this availability was abused by tenants. Treading the fine line between firmness and friendliness with tenants was a continual challenge which was not always confronted. Even the most able, calm staff could on occasions blow-up if the pressure became too great.

**Presence on the estate**

6.11   The advantages of having estate based staff could be seen on the experimental estates in both Tower Hamlets and Hull. Lifts out of order could be instantly reported and would affect staff as well as tenants. Poor cleaning was immediately reported by tenants if staff did not notice it. Squatters were reported at once. Noise nuisance could sometimes be dealt with at once by a visit. Workmen coming to the office could usually track down keys in order to get into property. Non-appearance by workmen was quickly reported, and staff heard from the repairmen if tenants were not in when they said they would be. These processes were more effective than in the more distant housing offices.

6.12   With an estate based office it was less easy for problems to be ignored or forgotten about. An example of this can be drawn from the smaller part of the control estate in Tower Hamlets which was a ten to fifteen minute walk from the housing office. These blocks were forgotten when bids for entry-phones were put forward. One property in the blocks had been identified at the start of the research period as a communal flat for elderly tenants to meet in. It was still boarded up at the end of the research. This kind of oversight was more difficult with on site staff.

6.13   However, simply basing staff on estates was not a solution to problems on its own. For instance, staff in Hull could have taken more initiatives to improve the cleanliness of the environment. Large items of rubbish could lie around for some time even by the main road into the estate without staff taking action. The fact that the Hull staff spent most of their time in the office meant that they were not always aware of physical problems on the estate.

**Size of office**

6.14   The level of decentralisation proposed by PEP entails the creation of much smaller offices than staff have been used to in centralised systems. Twenty staff was suggested by PEP as the right kind of size (this includes caretakers and repairmen). The Tower Hamlets experimental estate initially had three staff and a student, 3 local repairmen and four caretakers. Even when the estate was extended in 1988 there were only 5 office staff. So even by PEP standards this was a small office.

6.15　Certainly at the beginning of the research, the Tower Hamlets office was not coping. The level of commitment required by a staff of two to keep an office open was simply not present. Staff went out and did not commit themselves to coming back at a specific time. In addition, the Team Leader was frequently away and any holiday, training or other absence put impossible pressure on the member or members of staff remaining. The situation improved significantly when two more permanent staff were appointed and a good work atmosphere was created. Even so, occasionally, only one person was left to staff an open office and security became a problem at the end of the research.

6.16　Even in Hull, where the 5 staff members were much more office based, the odd occasion arose when only one member of staff was present. A minimum of five people seems to be necessary to keep an office open for any length of time on a regular basis. 7 or 8 staff makes the continuous administration of the office easier.

6.17　The other problem identified in Tower Hamlets was that expertise is not handed on when there is high staff turnover in small offices. A core of people who know what to do and what has happened previously do not exist. They move on so fast that knowledge and tradition is not handed on. Simple information about what had occurred previously did not seem to be known to new staff. The 100% turnover of staff on the Tower Hamlets experimental estate after 18 months meant previously built up contacts with tenants were treated like ancient history. We observed a PEP training meeting on monitoring. Two years later the administrator in the office had no idea that training had even taken place.

6.18　High turnover in small offices has to be addressed if local management is to work. Informal group memories have to be replaced by formal initial training and good record systems.

6.19　What does work well in small offices is communication. Staff know what has gone on because they cannot avoid hearing about it. We contrasted that level of intimacy with the central telephone repairs reporting service in Hull where much of the time the staff were wandering round asking who had taken a previous call and being unable to track down the first repairs reports to find out what they had done or why they had taken a certain decision.

**Computers**

6.20　Computers were a major advance, especially in repairs ordering when previously a large number of small jobs built up a huge mound of paper and were very hard to track manually. The computer system made "losing" jobs much harder. There were problems, too. Both PEP offices had micros on which repairs orders could be entered/printed and invoicing done. However, they were often out of action. Computer reliability and maintenance are crucial.

6.21　Both experimental offices were also linked to central computers. In Hull this was used for allocating tenants (which continued to be done city wide). Since April 1990 (October 1989 on the control estate) repairs ordering was centrally linked as well. This central linkage allows a centrally run system to be continued with decentralised offices. But if this is going to be the case, it is important that the lines are well maintained. The Hull experimental office was frequently unable to use its computer links for obtaining information on tenancies because lines were not working. The central system was slow and appeared unable to cope with the volume of work. A series of decentralised offices with central computer links requires sufficient computing staff being available to help remedy problems.

**Communications**

6.22 Central control of decentralised offices involves good traditional communication too! In Tower Hamlets the post was brought round every day to the offices and mail out was taken away. In Hull, this service was not available. The two PEP office team leaders decided they wanted to keep in regular contact with the centre and so they took it in turns to fetch the mail. Because the team leaders were the only members of the team with mileage allowances they undertook this work themselves - a waste of senior management time.

**Setting objectives for staff**

6.22 In a small office, distinctions between staff roles inevitably become blurred. Staff have to stand in for each other and cover a wider range of jobs than they would in a bigger office. The staff in the PEP offices tended to have wide job descriptions to allow for this.

6.23 A very wide job description can lead to dissatisfaction because staff felt they had never finished. In the study offices the lack of emphasis on monitoring performance meant that staff did not have a clear idea of the objectives that they were supposed to fulfil nor was there regular staff appraisal. In the Tower Hamlets experimental office, the manager offered staff a great deal of personal support and encouragement in an informal way. In the Tower Hamlets control office the team leader talked with staff about their ambitions within the job and helped them to obtain further training to enhance their performance and chances of promotion where they wanted it. In Hull there was little sense of this kind of management in either control or experimental office.

**Genericism**

6.24 Genericism in the local office was supported by PEP. A generic worker would provide all services to each tenant and thus avoid handing tenants round between staff. It also avoided demarcation disputes between staff. PEP was frequently criticised for this approach. Perhaps it was not altogether clear about whether it meant that all services should be provided by one person or that all services should be provided in one small local office by more specialist staff. In practice in a very small office, staff have to have generic skills because they will always be standing in for colleagues who are undertaking other jobs. The larger the office the more divided the jobs can be.

6.25 What a generic role does is to put more demands on the worker in organising his or her work load, working with a whole series of systems at one time rather than learning a small part of a system well. When a whole series of jobs has to be undertaken the less pleasant aspects (e.g. the policing side of rent arrears work) and the less clear cut parts (e.g. tenant liaison) tend to put to one side.

6.26 In our research, we saw no fully generic workers. We did see generic offices in Hull with virtually all services offered in the experimental office to tenants, except rent collection and Housing Benefit advice which arrived only later in the research period. The larger control office started to offer an almost complete service (apart from dealing with applications from homeless families) in October 1989. In London, allocations and Housing Benefit remained at Neighbourhood level in both offices, despite the local pilot in the experimental office. The experimental estate continued not to do arrears work. Early arrears work started to be undertaken in the control office in April 1990.

6.27 In practice a generic office rather than a generic worker seems to be what was aimed at. It may be that it is simpler for staff to work in this way. High staff turnover may mean it is better to restrict jobs so they can be learnt well in the short term. In a small office, it is hard for staff not to hear what is going on with other staff and tenants and this means inevitably that over lapping occurs and a personal service for tenants results even with specialist staff.

## Specialisation

6.28   Some work does seem to require speciality, e.g. Housing benefit, surveying and arrears work involving the courts. Even here there were differences between the estates on whether work was undertaken entirely by specialists or with some help from non-specialist workers. In the Tower Hamlets control estate, a technical officer took on much of the work involving repairs control, e.g. post repair inspections and some liaison on capital works. On the experimental estate, the team members undertook post repair inspections (later in the research period) and liaised with builders and surveyors on the capital works. A surveyor came regularly to the office for help with repairs and maintenance. In Hull, the Neighbourhood Assistants started to undertake post repair inspections of repairs after training and upgrading. But capital works were dealt with by a separate team and even tenant liaison was only partially supervised by the team leader.

6.29   Housing Benefit was a specialism in both Hull and Tower Hamlets and in both cases staff resisted the moves to decentralise it. But any staff dealing with arrears did need a knowledge of housing benefit work and in Hull a team leader criticised the Neighbourhood Housing Assistants for not knowing more. There is an uneasy tension between the need for a specialist in a complicated area of work and for the team members to know at least something about the work.

## Numbers of staff

6.30   PEP suggest a ratio of approximately 350 properties per generic housing officer. This is only a guide. In the Hull experimental estate there were 500 properties per Neighbourhood Housing Assistant, but there were more administrative staff than PEP suggested. Even with that level of staffing, staff were pressed. On the London experimental estate, however, there was one estate officer for 250 dwellings and an administrative officer. The London estate officers were not undertaking arrears work. Even so the staff were busy. This was partly because the repairs service was erratic and much time was spent chasing repairs. It was also partly because of the level of cover necessary for absence, holidays and training. This problem was dealt with during the research by the employment of two peripatetic relief staff for the whole Neighbourhood.

6.31   In short, the staff ratio suggested by PEP seems broadly to be correct as an average, but demands on staff alter depending on the effectiveness of other staff and the level of social and physical problems on the estate.

## In brief

6.32 ● The estate based offices did prove accessible and provided a friendly and broadly comprehensive service, especially in Hull.

● Some degree of specialism emerged in each office.

● The high demands put on the estate manager emphasised the case for good initial and recurrent training and senior officer support.

● Devolved responsibilities required new methods of monitoring standards and sustaining staff.

● Staffing levels suggested by PEP were broadly appropriate but staff were under considerable pressure and special circumstances could require extra help.

# Chapter 7

Tenant involvement in housing management

7.1    PEP did not spell out in its "Guide to Housing Management" the underlying reasons for its belief in tenant involvement in the running of estates. As we saw in Chapter One, the strong support for tenant involvement is grounded in the early work of the Priority Estates Project and in the experience of many of the PEP consultants. It was based on a belief that tenants rather than local authority officers were best able to identify deficiencies on the estates.

7.2    The PEP guide talks of "the intense sense of frustration at their own powerlessness that most residents' groups feel". To restore estates to an environment where people want to live involves giving power to those residents. Implicit in this thesis is a strong belief in the abilities of tenants both to take on responsibility communally and to understand and work with complex management issues. However, "Most tenants on run-down estates will not volunteer to take on full management responsibility. Many features are hard to manage and beyond their immediate control, such as rents, lettings, major repair, crime. Therefore, the landlord will have to forge a direct relationship with residents." (PEP Guide) Thus despite its attraction to the ideal of housing cooperatives, PEP has tended to emphasise "collaboration" and "consultation" at least as a first step. During the period of our research the 1988 Housing Act gave the opportunity for tenants to choose another landlord. In no case was this popular with tenants nor did any other landlord materialise wishing to take on any part of any of the estates. In London, opposition to the possibility was the only thing to attract widespread tenant interest. However, at the start of the research, the possibility of tenants choosing to move out of local authority ownership was very present in managers' minds and was a spur to change.

7.3    In practice, the thrust of PEP work has been to create a partnership between local authority housing managers and tenants. PEP found it hard to work with community workers who often favoured a combative approach towards the local authority rather than the cooperation PEP saw as essential. Most tenant consultation initially reveals a deep level of dissatisfaction. However, giving management responsibility to tenants means that the tenant body cannot simply be critical of management and councillors. The have to face the constraints too. One reason councillors gave for supporting tenant involvement in management, after experiencing it on the experimental estate in Hull, was that it meant that tenants came to understand the wider issues and constraints.

7.4    PEP is particularly concerned to promote consultation on day to day management, not just on the one off capital works which have usually been the subject of consultation. It is less easy for tenants to get involved in day to day management than with tangible issues like garden lay outs, windows or damp. Staff find it harder to appreciate the role tenants might play. Yet those consulted on capital works are often not the beneficiaries of the works given the long time lapse between applications for funding for capital works and the day the builders arrive on the estate.

7.5 PEP initially focused on tenant management cooperatives as the way for tenants to take control of management. As projects progressed it became clear that most tenants were not prepared to take on that level of responsibility. The Estate Management Board concept, created by two PEP consultants, gave tenants a lot of say without removing final responsibility from the local authority. This model was also more acceptable than tenant cooperatives to many councillors.

**Tenant involvement in practice**

7.6 Staff and tenants can interact at many levels. Frequently tenants are not even told about "improvements" that are to be made to the estate. The first they know is when the builders move onto the estate. On the other hand giving information can backfire. On the Tower Hamlets estate tenants were told when works were going to start but the contractors failed to turn up and this worked to the detriment of housing management staff's credibility. Conversely builders arrived on the estate without the prior knowledge of the housing staff.

7.7 On occasions tenants were consulted but then no account was taken of their opinions. On the Tower Hamlets experimental estate the PEP consultant consulted tenants (and caretakers) about improvements to the lifts before new lifts were installed. The suggestions made were carefully noted but the new lifts were the same as before and it appeared no notice whatsoever had been taken of local opinion.

7.8 In contrast we witnessed an extremely good programme of consultation on the Hull experimental estate. A booklet outlining the shape of the environmental changes and the kind of fencing and garden sheds that tenants might want was given to every household and interviews were conducted early in the research by housing staff and later by trainees to ascertain individual desires. To a very large extent these were met.

7.9 In Hull we also witnessed the creation of an Neighbourhood Management Committee where there had been no previous tenant activity in the area. We now look at the process in more detail.

**Implementation**
Hull

7.10 The major thrust of the PEP associate's work in Hull was to develop a tenant group. A copy book exercise of consultation was undertaken. (While there were two existing community organisations they were involved in the provision of services to pensioners and not with conditions on the estate.) Block meetings for the flats and area meetings for the rest of the estate were set up, both during the day and in the evenings. Council staff were not invited to these in order to allow tenants the freedom to say what they wanted. Tenants went through problems and issues on the estate. They were informed in their criticism by awareness of what had happened on the neighbouring PEP estate which already had a local office and a programme of improvements for the houses and the environment. That knowledge defined the solutions suggested by the tenants.

7.11 From each of these meetings tenants were asked if they would like to come to further meetings as representatives of their blocks and areas. There was considerable interest in this proposal. At further meetings, where Council staff were present, a steering group of tenants was set up. The roles they could play in running different models were described (Cooperative, Estate Management Board, sub-committee of the council, advisory group etc). The consultant presented the same options to councillors at a meeting in the Autumn of 1987 and they accepted that any of them would be possible.

However, when in 1988 the steering group decided it wanted to work towards an Estate Management Board, the councillors had second thoughts.

7.12   PEP for its part accepted that it had "moved the goal posts": when PEP was first involved in the estate there had been mention only of tenant participation and not tenant control of the management of the estate. Following representations from the central PEP directors to the chair of housing, councillors agreed to the setting up of a sub-committee of the housing committee with a majority of tenant representatives (who would be elected) plus the local councillors for the area. Tenants were unhappy about this change but agreed to it with the proviso that a review should be undertaken in two years time to discuss again a move to a more autonomous Estate Management Board. Exactly how the sub-committee would work in practice was still being debated at the end of the research period.

7.13   In September 1988, elections were held for the committee. There was a better turnout (about 35%) than in the local elections. Some of those elected had not been on the steering committee and needed the basic training that more established members had been receiving over the previous year and a half. This tenant training had covered both skills for running meetings and information on housing management with outside speakers, many provided by PEP. Tenants had made visits to other sites and PEP tenant conferences.

7.14   In addition to the Neighbourhood Management Committee, a tenants' association was set up and was given a temporary base in a house. It occupied rooms converted from bicycle sheds at the bottom of one of the central blocks of flats. The Tenants Association provided various services to tenants e.g. after school care for children, and a playgroup.

7.15   A PEP tenant liaison worker came into post in April 1989 and worked on both the Tenants Association development and that of the steering group and Neighbourhood Management Committee. He was also important in producing a regular newsletter and in setting up the election apparatus.

7.16   Only the Team Leader from the estate housing office staff was involved in contacts with the steering group and information was not given to staff on this aspect of the work on the estate. The Team Leader was involved in preparing early newsheets for the estate but on the whole he did not take initiatives on tenant activities partly because he was overwhelmed by the day to day management demands of the estate. No doubt these were increased by an increasingly assertive tenant group.

7.17   The other very successful aspect of tenant consultation concerned the environmental improvements. The estate staff were initially involved in this but withdrew once they moved into the estate office. The day to day consultation work was undertaken by two MSC funded trainees. The programme had already begun on the neighbouring PEP estate and continued in the same way. Three options for the houses were offered - one of which involved turning alternate rows of houses round so the houses no longer faced the backs of the next row of properties. This option was taken up by one group of tenants on the estate. It involved getting everyone in all the six rows to agree to the change and caused quite a few headaches. This scheme was very successful but the team decided it was really not possible to offer it elsewhere because of the cost and design difficulties. Nevertheless, there were choices to be made on fencing and sheds and size of gardens and tenants were pleased to make them.

7.18   In the blocks of flats consultation meetings were held but again the agenda had already been set in the neighbouring PEP estate. In the event, there was less money available for the research estate blocks but a similar kind of scheme was installed - creating meeting rooms in the base of blocks, installing video cameras and improving the door entry system, surrounding the blocks with fencing to limit access, and enhancing the environment.

7.19   In short, the experience in Hull has followed a text book pattern as laid down by PEP.

**Tower Hamlets**

7.20   In Tower Hamlets the PEP approach had a more mixed outcome with some successes and some failures.

7.21   When the research started the PEP consultant and the Estate Officer had already helped re-establish a moribund tenants association and it had coalesced around opposition to the housing management team acquiring the unused tenants' club room for its offices. In July 1987, the Tenants Association seemed well established with good relations with the PEP consultant. Meetings continued in an active way throughout the first year of the research. Complaints about caretaking brought changes, other non-local authority personnel came to explain the services provided on the estate (e.g. lift repair contractors). Tenant activities (e.g. children's football) were promoted on the estate. Members went on a PEP training course.

7.22   The PEP consultant established a PEP forum on the estate separate from the Tenants Association, although he and the management team attend meetings of both the forum and the Tenants' Association. The forum dealt specifically with housing matters while the TA focused on the wider life of the estate. The second team leader initially thought of setting up forums on the different parts of the estate but found that four groups took too much effort to create and sustain. She called one forum for the whole estate area once every six weeks which was only partially successful in bringing together representatives from all parts of the estate.

7.23   One of the most successful aspects was the creation of a Bengali group. This was largely the result of the work of the PEP consultant but the team leader worked cooperatively with him and it is instructive that it has been so successful. The fact that the consultant was of Indian origin was undoubtedly helpful in creating confidence. This Bengali group continued throughout the research period offering mutual support to the members of the Bengali community. Early on, it set up an after school "Muslim school" for the children. Bengali members continued to attend the main Tenants Association. It remains one of the most successful Bengali groups in the Neighbourhood which was previously an almost entirely white area.

7.24   However, the active, argumentative Tenants' Association was in regular conflict with the first estate office manager during the first year of the research. Frequent complaints were voiced to the PEP consultant. The team leader, for instance, decided the balconies of the two deck access blocks needed to be blocked off if any effective security system were to be installed. Some tenants were vehemently against this proposal. After a great deal of conflict a compromise plan was produced in which only some of the balconies were blocked.

7.25    In June 1988, because of the problems PEP had in dealing with the team leader, PEP decided to pull the consultant off the estate. This was done with no consultation with tenants. Some active members of the TA were by this time disillusioned with the whole effort and withdrew, others moved. When the new team leader started in September, the TA was no longer functioning effectively.

7.26    The PEP consultant was replaced by a PEP tenant liaison worker who was Bengali. He offered some help to the main Tenants' Association. But the main thrust of his work was with the Bengali group.

7.27    The Tenants' Association had some revival. However, while one of the tenants' groups in the Neighbourhood was setting up an Estate Management Board, the tenants on the experimental estate were finding it hard to organise tenants meetings at the end of the research. Tenants associations on other parts of the estate have had mixed success as well. On the older block 10 minutes from the main estate, the tenant mix has helped give the estate the skills to run a TA and this has continued to function. A PEP survey of the extra part of the estate (added in September 1988) led to the formation of an active tenants association there.

7.28    Consultations on capital works had a patchy history too. A plan by a landscape architect for the area in 1987 was not accepted by a tenants' meeting. Tenants felt they were consulted only once the plan was drawn up and not before. A survey had taken place but no results were ever produced. It was hard to discover what had happened. The landscape architect sat in a flat at certain times and invited tenants to see the plan but few came and he felt disillusioned. He was regarded with scorn by the housing management team because he did not want to work in the evenings. The new estate manager went ahead with the plan assuming tenants had agreed to it. By then there was no tenants' group to disillusion her.

7.29    The landscape architect said tenants had been consulted on adding gardens to one older block in 1986 but when they had been installed no one gardened and tenants now claimed they had never wanted gardens.

7.30    In July 1988, the Neighbourhood Housing Manager and the Estate Officer stepped into the breach left by the absence of the first team leader and consulted tenants on a series of small schemes that could sit on the shelf and be ready in case money suddenly became available at the end of a financial year.

7.31    When the new team leader arrived she altered the security plan, saving money in order to be able to add gates and gateways to the whole estate. This was initiated by her not by tenants, though the ailing tenants' group was consulted.

7.32    Additional capital resources provided new lifts in the deck access blocks and central heating in many of the older blocks. The PEP consultant had been strongly against the installation of new lifts before security work had been completed on the block entrances because of vandalism. This proved a well justified fear.

7.33    In March 1990, a tenant liaison worker was appointed to work for three months with tenants on the major rehabilitation of one of the oldest blocks on the estate. Much of this work involved liaising with the contractor and discussing with tenants the level of compensation paid to them for the disruption they were suffering.

7.34   During the research period only one news sheet was produced for tenants. It was not well done (some of it came from an earlier published news sheet and was not relevant) and much of the language used was academic.

7.35   In brief, beyond the initiation of the Bengali group on the Tower Hamlets estate little meaningful tenant involvement occurred.

## Some conclusions

Tenant management is not easy

7.36   These accounts are further proof, if any were needed, that the exercise of the "voice" option by consumers is not easy or costless.

7.37   After three years of intensive work in Hull, PEP had set up a solid base on which to build tenant involvement. Even so it is too early to say how this will work in the longer term. There was no base in Hull on which the PEP consultant could build. The experience on other PEP estates where there was already an active tenants group was different. An active tenants' group could take on housing management issues. To set up a group from scratch is a long term venture. The level of training and support needed by tenants is considerable especially where few participating tenants have skills for running a meeting.

7.38   In Tower Hamlets, the withdrawal of the PEP consultant coincided with its decision to support an Estate Management Board on one of the other Neighbourhood bases and PEP decided to concentrate its efforts there. Although PEP continued to give some support on the experimental estate it was not intensive. Because of the lack of responsiveness of the first team leader to the tenants the initial enthusiasm of tenants on the experimental estate had waned and indeed turned to cynicism. The new team leader who was working with less PEP help had more to do than if no work had been undertaken with the tenants previously. While she took the need for tenant consultation seriously, working with the tenants' group was not her top priority. She tended to consult individual tenants. More of her energy was used to make contacts with those outside the estate who could help, work on Neighbourhood housing issues, and the promotion of the training centre rather than work on the creation of a solid tenant group.

7.39   If tenant participation is to be taken seriously it involves significant management attention at senior level and PEP really failed to graft this onto the prevailing local authority managers' view.

7.40   In Hull a good job had been done but it had not been achieved by the busy housing manager who had his hands full. The task fell almost exclusively to the PEP consultant.

7.41   Work with tenants is time consuming and a skilled task. It cannot simply be tacked on to a busy housing manager role, especially when major changes like capital works are in prospect and are likely to capture the manager's attention.

7.42   On the London **control** estate the manager had previously worked in an authority which put tenant participation high on the agenda for housing managers. This officer, with her senior's support, worked successfully with various tenants' groups. She had firstly, experience, and secondly a strong commitment to the idea of tenant involvement in the management function. She frequently worked overtime outside office hours to fulfil that part of her job. (So too did the manager on the experimental estate but on different issues.) However, to expect all managers to add on to a full day, evening meetings which can be both stressful and critical of their work, is unrealistic.

**Tenant resources**

7.43   On the other hand, involvement in management can unlock personal resources in the tenants.

7.44   As one tenant in Hull said, "If you had told me three years ago that I would be chairing a meeting of 250 people, I would never have believed it".

7.45   The research also showed that it is possible to set up an active tenants' group which is interested and able to be involved in management decisions even on estates with terrible reputations. In Hull there was widespread prejudice against the experimental estate, as we saw. This was shared by ordinary Hull citizens and some staff in the housing department. Some councillors were surprised at the level of interest and ability of the tenants on the experimental estate. Promoting a tenants' group and interaction with it requires particular managerial qualities and training. Yet there remains an uneasy relationship between the tenants, the staff and the councillors. For the manager on-going interaction is demanding. Decision making power has moved from the centre to the estate manager, only to be constrained by the instruction to consult the tenant body. The more dynamic the managers, the more likely they are to feel constrained by the time and effort required to get results. For a manager to work constructively with tenants, and not to feel constrained demands high qualities and good training. Tenants groups can be difficult and unconstructive. Thinking in a vague kind of way that participation is a good thing, will not carry a manager through. The culture within a housing department has to strongly favour tenant involvement or to have continuous pressure from outside if it is to take root.

7.46   One manager spoke positively about tenant participation as a way of spreading democracy. That kind of belief seemed necessary to give managers the perseverance to carry on. The PEP consultants had that level of belief necessary to pursue tenant participation through many vicissitudes. Managers brought up in local authority service may not have that level of conviction or training in handling groups.

**Councillors and tenants can learn to work together**

7.47   Councillors largely welcomed tenant participation. They could have seen tenant management as a diminution in their own power to represent tenants' interests. But most saw tenant participation as a positive move. In Hull, where there seemed to be little tradition of tenant interaction with the Council, the change for both tenants and councillors was great. The experience on the two neighbouring PEP estates seemed to have impressed councillors enough to want to extend, at least some tenant participation to the new Neighbourhood committees which were set up as part of the decentralisation programme.

**Tenants too need training**

7.48   Tenants for their part had to learn how to interact with Councillors and housing managers in a new way. The new manager in Hull was trying to wean Neighbourhood Management Committee members away from always asking for him in the office and not going through office staff when that was possible. Tenants need to learn not just technical matters, such as the way local authorities and local budgets work, but about the proper boundaries of their work and how to be effective representatives. It is not enough just to provide training when the Committee is set up. New members need initial training and continuing ones need more advanced opportunities. They also require independent advice.

**"Voice" versus "Exit"**

7.49 Economists argue that "voice", preferences expressed through representative institutions, are a weak form of pressure. The sanctions of "exit" provided by the normal market are much more effective (Hirschman 1970). Consumer involvement in decision making is costly and relatively ineffective. This research suggests that it is, indeed, difficult to do well. It also shows that for estates like this there is really little alternative. Realistically, most tenants have little chance of exit. Even when they do leave it does not pose a threat to the staff or an incentive for better service. On the contrary it worsens the situation, demoralising the staff. The estate officers do not face bankruptcy as a spur to action if they fail. Compulsory tendering is not likely to attract eager bidders to administer poor estates. Learning how to make the tenant voice count is the only realistic option for such deprived estates. As this research shows, it can be done.

# Part Three

## THE OUTCOMES

## Chapter 8 — Quality of life on the estates

**Tenants' views**

8.1    The prediction made by the advocates of estate based management was that it would improve tenants' quality of life and their satisfaction with the estate. This would be achieved most directly by the improved efficiency with which the caretaking, cleaning, repairs and lettings functions were carried out. The most obvious way to measure tenants' views about their quality of life was to ask them about it. The Tenant Survey did this, repeating the same questions to tenants in June 1990 as were asked in June 1987. Tenants on the control estates were asked the same core questions as those on the experimental estates.

**Tenants' attitudes**

8.2    Tenants were asked a series of questions about their environment. The first was a very general one about their satisfaction with their estate. The greatest dissatisfaction before the experiment began was expressed by the residents on the experimental estate in Hull (see Table 8.1).

*Table 8.1*    **Satisfaction with estate (percentages)**

|  | Hull | | | | London | | | |
|---|---|---|---|---|---|---|---|---|
|  | Experimental | | Control | | Experimental | | Control | |
|  | Before | After | Before | After | Before | After | Before | After |
| Very or fairly satisfied | 45 | 54 | 63 | 65 | 52 | 68 | 54 | 64 |
| Neither satisfied nor dissatisfied | 11 | 9 | 13 | 7 | 12 | 9 | 18 | 15 |
| Very or fairly dissatisfied | 43 | 37 | 24 | 28 | 36 | 23 | 28 | 21 |
| Not stated | 1 | | - | | - | | - | |
| Base No | 578 | 573 | 480 | 496 | 242 | 268 | 382 | 392 |

Source: *Tenants Survey 1987, 1990*

8.3    43% said they were very or fairly dissatisfied with the estate. After three years the number expressing dissatisfaction had decreased to 37% and the satisfied figure had risen from 45% to 54%. It has to be remembered that to tenants "the estate" in Hull tends to mean Orchard Park as a whole. This was a weakness in the specificity of the original questionnaire. It is also important to remember that, as we have seen, only part of the experimental area had been physically improved at the time of the second survey. Nevertheless, the improved satisfaction rating contrasts with a slightly worsened score on the control estate. The percentage expressing dissatisfaction rose by 2% there.

8.4    Much more striking were the responses to the question as to whether tenants thought the estate had **improved** in the past two to three years (see Table 8.2).

*Table 8.2*  **Whether estate has improved in the last 2/3 years**
           **(percentages)**

|  | Hull | | | | London | | | |
|  | Experimental | | Control | | Experimental | | Control | |
|  | Before | After | Before | After | Before | After | Before | After |
|---|---|---|---|---|---|---|---|---|
| Improved | 3 | 27 | 6 | 13 | 19 | 51 | 10 | 29 |
| Got worse | 61 | 38 | 39 | 38 | 26 | 13 | 32 | 15 |
| Stayed same | 28 | 22 | 49 | 41 | 44 | 28 | 48 | 45 |
| Don't know | 7 | 13 | 6 | 9 | 12 | 7 | 10 | 11 |

Source and base numbers: *As for Table 8.1*

8.5   In 1987 61% thought the estate had got worse in the past few years. In 1990, on the experimental estate only 38% thought so and 27% thought it had got better - a view held by only 3% three years earlier. Some people on the control estate also felt things had improved but 79% thought it had stayed the same or got worse and 9% did not know.

8.6   In London both estates showed an improved satisfaction score but the experimental estate showed the greatest improvement, the dissatisfied tenants showed the biggest drop on the experimental estate. No fewer than 51% thought the estate had got better.

8.7   On the Hull estate where the environmental work was in progress the level of optimism was high. 44% thought that things would improve. On the control estate the comparable figure was only 10%. On the London estate the local team and PEP had done preliminary work with tenants before the survey took place in 1987 and expectations had been raised. Thus 34% thought there would be an improvement in June 1987. Only 28% thought there would be further improvements in 1990. This no doubt also reflects the degree of disillusion brought about by the false start to the project and the removal of the first manager. More people on the control estate expected there would be improvements (see Table 8.3).

*Table 8.3*  **Whether estate will improve in the next 2 years (percentages)**

|  | Hull | | | | London | | | |
|  | Experimental | | Control | | Experimental | | Control | |
|  | Before | After | Before | After | Before | After | Before | After |
|---|---|---|---|---|---|---|---|---|
| Improve | 19 | 44 | 12 | 10 | 34 | 28 | 30 | 47 |
| Get worse | 46 | 20 | 40 | 31 | 18 | 17 | 18 | 10 |
| Stay same | 27 | 23 | 35 | 40 | 31 | 28 | 21 | 21 |
| Don't know | 8 | 13 | 13 | 19 | 17 | 27 | 31 | 22 |

Source and base numbers: *As for Table 8.1*

8.8   Perhaps the greatest set back for the original PEP model, however, was that despite the evident improvements which tenants recognised, the numbers wishing to **move** had fallen very little. The impact on tenants' desire to stay on the estates despite their perceived improvements, was not great in Hull (Table 8.4).

*Table 8.4* **Percentage of households who would choose to move/stay, if had a choice**

| | Hull | | | | London | | | |
| | Experimental | | Control | | Experimental | | Control | |
| | Before | After | Before | After | Before | After | Before | After |
| --- | --- | --- | --- | --- | --- | --- | --- | --- |
| Stay | 41 | 44 | 50 | 48 | 24 | 44 | 40 | 43 |
| Move | 53 | 49 | 42 | 47 | 63 | 46 | 48 | 45 |
| It depends | 5 | 6 | 7 | 4 | 11 | 8 | 11 | 11 |
| Don't know | 1 | 2 | 1 | 2 | 1 | 2 | 1 | 2 |

Source and base numbers: *As for Table 8.1*

8.9 The site, its inconvenience and the attitudes to it as part of the much larger estate no doubt explain this. However, slightly more tenants wanted to stay at the end of the three year period on the experimental estate and slightly fewer on the control estate. The percentage requesting transfers remained the same (Table 8.5).

*Table 8.5* **Percentage of households that had requested a transfer**

| Hull | | | | London | | | |
| Experimental | | Control | | Experimental | | Control | |
| Before | After | Before | After | Before | After | Before | After |
| --- | --- | --- | --- | --- | --- | --- | --- |
| 32 | 32 | 27 | 25 | 39 | 26 | 38 | 43 |

Source and base numbers: *As for Table 8.1*

8.10 In London a strikingly larger group wished to stay on the experimental estate at the end of the research, despite its less desirable siting in relation to the City. 44% instead of 24% wanted to remain. The control estate showed a very small increase in the number wanting to stay of 3%. Significantly fewer families were requesting transfers on the experimental estate - 26% down from 39%.

8.11 A more detailed analysis of complaints about the estates may well reflect a heightened degree of expectation engendered by tenant participation especially in Hull. This shows up in the increased complaints that there are insufficient safe play areas, for example (see Table 8.6).

8.12 There is some improvement in the views expressed that rubbish and litter are a "Big Problem" in the Hull estate but many of the other specific issues remain a problem on both estates despite improvements.

8.13 The substantial increases in tenants saying that they were worried by noisy people and people hanging around in the Hull experimental site reflect the new allocations policy and the trouble in the flats that we discuss later in the chapter.

8.14 In the London experimental estate there had been a marked improvement in the number of tenants worried about litter, dogs, graffiti, broken windows and doors, lifts that did not work, dirty communal areas, lighting empty houses, car parking, and abandoned cars. However, improvements had also taken place on the control estate, according to the tenants. This applied to fewer broken windows and doors, dirty common areas and above all disturbance by teenagers. Rubbish and litter and lifts had improved little.

**Table 8.6   Percentage of respondents for each estate that said item was a 'big problem' on the estate**

| | Hull | | | | London | | | |
|---|---|---|---|---|---|---|---|---|
| | Experimental | | Control | | Experimental | | Control | |
| | Before | After | Before | After | Before | After | Before | After |
| Lack of safe play areas for children | 53 | 61 | 42 | 47 | 31 | 32 | 27 | 48 |
| Rubbish and litter lying around | 72 | 67 | 58 | 70 | 35 | 25 | 39 | 36 |
| Dogs | 66 | 58 | 53 | 67 | 45 | 20 | 18 | 21 |
| Graffiti | 53 | 50 | 28 | 24 | 26 | 19 | 32 | 28 |
| Broken windows | 33 | 32 | 14 | 25 | 20 | 14 | 30 | 15 |
| Broken doors | 21 | 20 | 8 | 11 | 20 | 13 | 21 | 10 |
| Lifts that don't work | 19 | 25 | 2 | – | 45 | 10 | 37 | 35 |
| Dirty communal areas i.e. stairs, hallways, lifts | 21 | 21 | 6 | 2 | 48 | 23 | 48 | 38 |
| Broken lighting in stairs, hallways, lifts | 11 | 15 | 4 | 1 | 16 | 9 | 15 | 10 |
| Broken street lighting | 13 | 15 | 5 | 7 | 6 | 5 | 5 | 4 |
| Empty houses/flats | 28 | 23 | 11 | 16 | 14 | 5 | 10 | 4 |
| Secure car-parking | 45 | 50 | 24 | 25 | 23 | 11 | 30 | 17 |
| Disturbance from teenagers or youths | 42 | 44 | 24 | 26 | 16 | 12 | 22 | 7 |
| Noisy parties | 8 | 13 | 2 | 4 | 7 | 6 | 5 | 3 |
| Noisy neighbours apart from teenagers | 10 | 15 | 8 | 8 | 5 | 9 | 8 | 4 |
| Noisy people outside your home | 21 | 33 | 11 | 15 | 10 | 9 | 12 | 5 |
| People mending cars and bikes outside your home | 12 | 7 | 4 | 6 | 6 | 4 | 4 | 2 |
| Broken down and abandoned cars | 6 | 3 | 1 | 2 | 9 | 2 | 5 | 3 |
| People who say insulting things or bother people as they walk down the streets | 13 | 16 | 7 | 8 | 5 | 4 | 3 | 2 |
| People using illegal drugs | 9 | 18 | 11 | 10 | 2 | 3 | 4 | 2 |
| Speeding traffic | 29 | 39 | 18 | 20 | 24 | 22 | 16 | 7 |
| People hanging around drinking | 25 | 41 | 6 | 10 | 8 | 5 | 4 | 2 |

Source: *As Table 8.1*

**Fear of crime and crime**

8.15   Tenants fear of crime decreased on the experimental estate in Hull but sharply increased on the control estate (Table 8.7).

8.16   The improvements, providing fences and closing off access, though not yet fully in place, had helped affect fear of crime.

*Table 8.7*   **Percentage of respondents who were 'very worried' about particular crimes**

| | Hull | | | | London | | | |
|---|---|---|---|---|---|---|---|---|
| | Experimental | | Control | | Experimental | | Control | |
| | Before | After | Before | After | Before | After | Before | After |
| Having home broken into and something stolen | 50 | 45 | 40 | 58 | 45 | 32 | 56 | 28 |
| Having your home or property damaged by vandals | 47 | 40 | 35 | 50 | 40 | 29 | 51 | 24 |
| Being attacked or robbed while on the estate | 43 | 37 | 36 | 45 | 38 | 25 | 47 | 22 |

**Source:** As for Table 8.1

8.17   These perceptions reflected real changes. The crime questions on the Tenant Survey reported by Hope and Foster (1993) show that there was a significant reduction in burglary on the Hull experimental estate relative to the control estate and a smaller relative increase in car thefts. Other offences rose in line with the control estate.

8.18   Fear of crime on both estates in London had fallen. Indeed it had fallen faster on the control estate than on the experimental. Fear of crime had been greater on the control estate to begin with and was similar but slightly lower than the experimental estate at the end of the research period.

8.19   Again these figures reflect reported rates of victimisation. Hope and Foster (1991) report that rates of victimisation on the London PEP estate for household offences declined by 26%. This was especially noticeable in the case of burglary which declined by 55%. Reductions were even greater on the control estate - household offences down 50% and down 79% in burglaries.

8.20   Hope and Foster speculate that one reason for this may be the stabilisation of the community in the period of the research, notably the Bengali population. An articulate tenant group emerged, local police noted the greater solidarity of the Asian youth, and racially motivated crime reduced more on the control estate. The Asian group was larger and more settled on the control estate. Thus, in many ways the control estate worked much more like a PEP estate was supposed to do. But that had a lot to do with the long term social dynamics of the area. There was also in place, it should be remembered, a decentralised and well run, if not estate based, form of housing management.

**In brief**

8.21   Tenants on both experimental estates thought the quality of life had improved and improved more than on the control estates. This was most strikingly true in Hull where the PEP approach had been most fully implemented.

8.22 Reductions in crime and fear of crime had improved most on the experimental estate in Hull where most had been done to combat it through improvements to the estate and through work with tenants in general. Thus far the model could be said to have been sustained. The small reductions in tenants' desire to move off the Hull experimental estate and the big improvements to crime rates on the London control estate, however, show how important other basic social forces were.

# Chapter 9

# The environment measured

9.1   Tenants' attitudes to their environment may not be only a reflection of real change. They may be affected by changing expectations. It was considered important to try to measure as objectively as possible the actual environmental changes that had occurred on each estate at regular intervals.

9.2   It was necessary to begin by finding out what aspects of the physical environment tenants thought important so as not to impose the researchers' prejudices on the measures adopted. This had been one of the criticisms levelled at Coleman's (1985) work.

9.3   The Tenant Survey was taken as the starting point. The 1987 survey results gave a clear indication of those things that tenants saw as a "big problem" on their estates. The items that were directly related to the physical environment were noted. The one with the highest score was "rubbish and litter lying around". Other items were uncontrolled dogs, graffiti, broken windows and doors, dirty communal areas, empty houses and flats, broken lighting, lack of secure car parking and safe play areas. So far as possible these complaints were translated into a defined nuisance, such as the extent of rubbish, graffiti and damage to communal doors, broken windows and so on. An observer rating score was developed for each of these nuisances. Sample areas were then chosen and an observer was asked to record the existence of such a nuisance at that site once every three months. To make the indicator more sensitive the rating scale recorded not just the existence of litter or rubbish but the extent of it. For example, on a site like a common staircase, the observer was asked to record whether there was no rubbish, minor quantities of, for example, cigarette packets or fast food boxes, larger items like sacks of rubbish, and finally very large items like a chair, mattress or similar bulky objects. After several pilot surveys and checks using independent observers the scoring methods were judged reliable. Untrained observers got within 5% of most of the scores. In fact, one skilled observer undertook all the surveys in the three years.

9.4   Sample sites were chosen in all the blocks and areas within the experimental and control estates.

9.5   Total possible scores were derived from each area and compared to the actual scores. A score of 100% for an estate would mean that every site sampled would have serious rubbish with large items also in evidence, extensive graffiti, broken common doors, flats boarded up, windows broken and faeces lying about. No 100% scores were recorded but some blocks did score nearly 50% on some occasions which bespeaks a fairly appalling quality of life in those blocks. All the estates began with scores in the 25-30% range.

9.6   The difference between the actual absolute raw scores on different estates should not be taken as significant. The essential comparison was with the same estate over time. Did its environmental score change? Did it change more or less than its comparable estate?

9.7    The base line for the London estates was January 1988 when both estates were surveyed together for the first time and July 1988 in Hull.

9.8    Following Newman (1972) the sample areas were distinguished according to the extent of public access they had. Thus "public space" was commonly used by large numbers of people gaining access to a whole block . "Semi public space" included deck access to a range of dwellings, "semi private areas" referred, for example, to the space on the landing onto which no more than four dwellings opened. "Private space" included the dwellings' own garden. For a full description of the survey method see the Appendix.

9.9    The prediction from the model in Chapter Two was that levels of rubbish and graffiti and other damage to public areas would decline as the localised caretaking service and repairs teams got to work. This would be most apparent in the flats where there were common public areas and in tower blocks and deck access blocks especially. In Hull the wide open areas and two storey terrace housing would be less responsive; they merely had a handy man to help tidy the open areas. There the enclosure of the common areas and the creation of private gardens would be the expected change factor. So too would be possible improved attitudes to the estate generated by the tenant consultation process.

9.10    Unfortunately the doors and entry phone system that were to have been installed in the deck access block on the London experimental estate were still not there at the end of the research. Any improvement here would be the result of management alone.

**The results of the environmental survey**

The London experimental estate

9.11    As Table 9.1, indicates the scores for rubbish, graffiti and internal property damage on the experimental estate in January 1988 were all near, or over, the 30% mark indicating a serious environmental problem. External property damage was almost as high at 27% Litter and uncut grass on the large open areas in the middle of the estate and elsewhere scored 14%. The garages were also fairly heavily damaged, scoring 20%. The other percentage scores appear much lower but they refer to the proportion of all houses and flats that had windows or doors broken or boarded up.

9.12    The pilot surveys prior to January on Robin Hood Gardens suggest that the efforts by the PEP consultant to work with the caretakers to improve the caretaking function did produce results temporarily but things returned to normal by the time the January survey was undertaken.

9.13    After the estate office opened in the Autumn of 1987 there was a small improvement in the rubbish, graffiti and damage indicators in early 1988. These were reversed in July and October. It will be recalled that that was the period when the estate office ceased to function properly and was often closed. In the Autumn of 1988 a new manager was appointed who began to work effectively with the local caretaking team. After July 1988 the indicators begin to show a long term improvement. The rubbish score falls thereafter fairly steadily and by the time of the last survey in June 1990 it had fallen to 60. That is a fall of about 40% (see Figure 9.1).

*Table 9.1*  **Environmental scores (percentages): London experimental and control estates**

**Actual damage of any given type as % of potential damage of any given type**

|  | 1988 | | | | 1989 | | | | 1990 | | |
|---|---|---|---|---|---|---|---|---|---|---|---|
|  | Jan | Apr | Jul | Oct | Jan | Apr | Jul | Oct | Jan | Apr | Jun |
| **London experimental estate** | | | | | | | | | | | |
| Rubbish | 29 | 24 | 26 | 25 | 21 | 23 | 23 | 23 | 20 | 18 | 17 |
| Graffiti | 32 | 33 | 34 | 36 | 27 | 27 | 27 | 31 | 25 | 25 | 26 |
| Internal damage | 32 | 34 | 28 | 29 | 26 | 28 | 30 | 30 | 29 | 29 | 27 |
| External damage | 27 | 23 | 27 | 22 | 15 | 22 | 27 | 24 | 26 | 18 | 27 |
| Open spaces | 14 | 28 | 9 | 4 | 2 | 9 | 8 | 8 | 3 | 6 | 5 |
| **Percentage of units affected** | | | | | | | | | | | |
| Windows boarded | 4 | 5 | 4 | 3 | 2 | 3 | 4 | 3 | 9 | 1 | 1 |
| Doors boarded | 0.9 | 1.5 | 0.9 | 0.2 | 2.3 | 1.9 | 1.9 | 1.8 | 0.7 | 0.5 | 0.9 |
| Garages damaged | 20 | 23 | 14 | 6 | 2 | 2 | 4 | 1 | 2 | 2 | 1 |
| **London control estate** | | | | | | | | | | | |
| Rubbish | 23 | 29 | 28 | 24 | 27 | 24 | 28 | 23 | 17 | 22 | 21 |
| Graffiti | 40 | 50 | 52 | 44 | 49 | 50 | 42 | 44 | 42 | 42 | 43 |
| Internal damage | 43 | 45 | 45 | 45 | 36 | 37 | 30 | 33 | 31 | 32 | 34 |
| External damage | 21 | 24 | 23 | 20 | 19 | 21 | 22 | 21 | 25 | 25 | 19 |
| Open spaces | 22 | 28 | 18 | 20 | 4 | 20 | 10 | 12 | 13 | 13 | 22 |
| **Percentage of units affected** | | | | | | | | | | | |
| Windows boarded | 8 | 7 | 5 | 5 | 11 | 3 | 2 | 4 | 5 | 4 | 5 |
| Doors boarded | 1.5 | 1.9 | 2.5 | 1.0 | 0.5 | 1.7 | 0.5 | 0.5 | 0.5 | 1.0 | 1.0 |
| Garages damaged | 14 | 9 | 10 | 5 | 1 | 3 | 4 | 6 | 2 | 0 | 0 |

*Figure 9.1*  **Changes in environmental nuisance scores: London experimental estate**

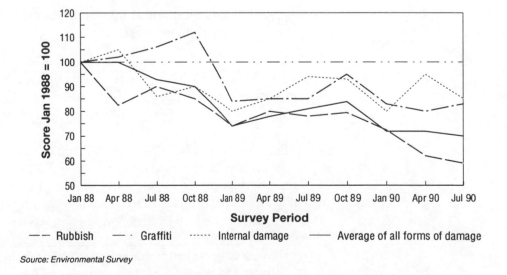

— — Rubbish    — · Graffiti    ······ Internal damage    —— Average of all forms of damage

*Source: Environmental Survey*

9.14  Since, as we saw earlier, the main blocks were not secured, most of this improvement has to be put down to the close supervision the estate manager was able to give to the caretaking function in the estate office and by being on site. A striking improvement in the care of the open grassed areas was also achieved. The least satisfactory change relates to the external property damage which it could be argued is likely to be least responsive to caretaking or repairs work. Structural works aimed at making damage to the external fabric more difficult were unfinished when the research ended.

9.15   In Figure 9.1 we show the trends in the major indicators over the study period. The base line of 100 refers to the scores at January 1988. Subsequent scores are then related to that base. The overall average gives an equal weight to rubbish, graffiti, internal damage and to a combined figure for all other forms of nuisance. The overall average for the experimental estate falls by thirty percent from January 1988 to June 1990. The general trend has been down though there was some worsening in mid 1989. Internal damage and graffiti have been most resistant to change but the scale of improvement is significant in relation to the margins of error with which we began.

9.16   A block by block analysis of the indicators suggests that where external work had been done on entry doors to the blocks this did make a difference. The blocks affected were those on the oldest and most dilapidated parts of the estate on which work began first. Work was completed on Block 9 in June 1989. This was one of the worst blocks having an average score of 35% at the outset which came down to 17% by the end of the research. This is still not a pleasant environment but was a major improvement. Graffiti and internal damage rise again after the initial work but rubbish and other damage is contained and the overall average is kept level over that subsequent year. Major improvements were achieved on Block 10, though structural changes were only just complete in June 1990. Blocks 12 and 13 on which work had been completed earlier showed large improvements - 60% and 50% starting from very poor original environments.

9.17   An analysis of the results by the type of space involved is instructive and re-enforces these findings. The caretakers and managers could be expected to have most effect on the public spaces over which they had direct responsibility. All these scores improve dramatically (see Figure 9.2). The same is true for rubbish in the semi public areas. This suggests that the cleaning and oversight duties in the more public areas do explain the overall improvements.

*Figure 9.2*   **Environmental nuisance scores: public space only - London experimental estate**

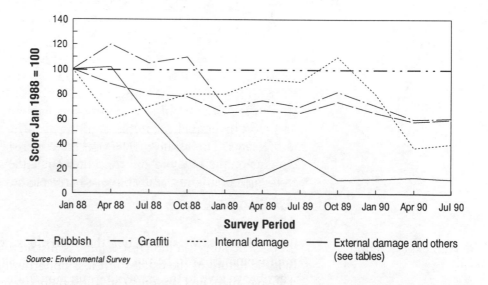

Source: Environmental Survey

**The London control estate**

9.18   The control estate showed much less change. The trend for rubbish and litter on the estate rises and then falls back to a score not very different to the first level. The extent of graffiti which had a score of nearly 40 at the outset rose at several points to 50 or more and then fell to a figure in excess of the original level. The estate average for internal property damage did fall but was associated with the major capital work undertaken on one block that was in our sample ( see below). There was some reduction in external property damage and fewer properties with windows broken or boarded up but there was no change in the general appearance of the open areas. The one dramatic improvement came in the underground garages which had been sold off to a private company and came to be used by office workers in the nearby printing offices. The overall average score showed a small fall from nearly 29 to 26% and nearly all that is the result of enclosure and security work on the one tower block. Ex GLC money, originally intended for several blocks, was amalgamated to make a thorough job on this one block. The entire lobby areas were completely remodelled, access ramps were removed, entrances redesigned, internal doors replaced and lifts replaced. As a result the average damage score dropped by more than half, though the rubbish level did not (Block 4). Without that capital work the average score on the estate would have remained static or worse at various points through the study period. Two smaller blocks had entry phones installed and one had lifts replaced. Other work, mainly covering graffiti with a coat of paint, was undertaken in some of the worst blocks but it produced no lasting effect. See Figure 9.3 for a comparison of the average scores on the two estates.

*Figure 9.3*  **Environmental nuisance scores**

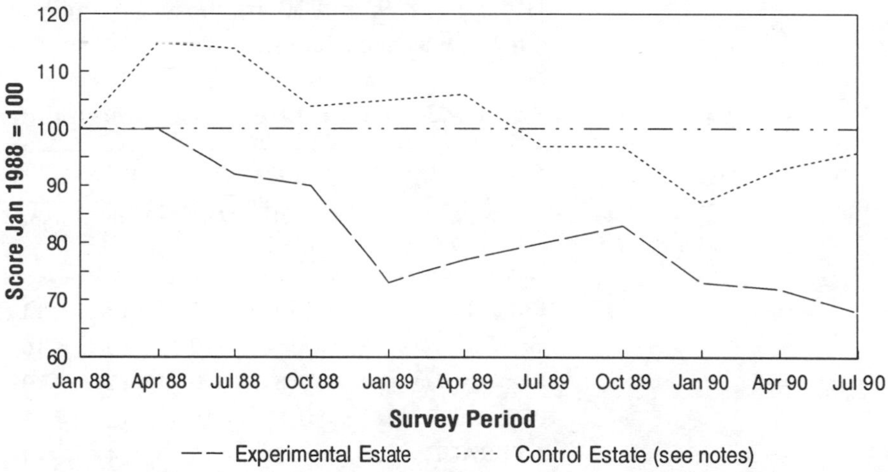

Source: Environmental Survey          One block excluded on Control Estate where environment work was undertaken

9.19   The control estate had an experienced and very dedicated manager running a local but not estate based office, as we have explained. He tried to keep on top of the caretaking and cleaning functions. But he was not on the spot. It is difficult not to draw the conclusion that the very fact of proximity and close oversight made the significant difference we observe between the two estates. The estate officers on the experimental estate saw the litter and damage on their way to and from the office, they were on the receiving end of frequent complaints and above all it was their environment as well as the tenants'.

The Hull experimental estate

9.20   The story on the Hull estates is instructive in a different way. We saw that the nature of the estates left less opportunity for the caretaking role to be decisive than in London. The flats there were better cared for before the experiment began. The environmental work on the experimental estate was only half complete by the end of the project and where building work was in process the environment had deteriorated in the meantime, because of the work.

9.21 The overall average and the component indicators for the Hull experimental estate show little change and some slight worsening over the period of the study (see Table 9.2). The environmental damage score rises from 12.0% to 12.9%.

The Hull control estate

9.22 The control estate shows little change and again a slight worsening. The score rose over the period from 14.2% to 14.7% with periods during which the average score rose to 15%. The average experience of the two estates seems very similar (see Figure 9.4). However, once the analysis is undertaken at a block or on a small area basis the picture changes. The control estate is mostly unchanging throughout with three areas showing significant worsening. On the experimental estate there is a very clear divergence in the scores by small area or "Thorpe". Those Thorpes on which environmental works had been undertaken, before the final survey was administered, showed major improvements in their scores. The Thorpe on which the work was first complete, Dodthorpe, showed an average score for rubbish, graffiti and property damage which was 14.8 in July 1988 which rose to 19.9 in the autumn of 1988, but then fell when the work was completed and was 4.9 when the final survey was undertaken nine months after the work on fencing and private gardens was complete (see Figure 9.5). The score on Easthorpe began at 14.8 and rose at one point to 25.3. After the changes we have described the score fell to 5.7 in June 1990. Gorthorpe, comprising roughly half flats and half houses, reached 16.6 at one early point but fell to 2.7 after environmental work was completed. Blocks 7, 8, 9, and 10 are those on which work was completed before the last survey was undertaken.

*Table 9.2* **Hull estates environmental percentages (scores out of 100)**

| | 1988 | | 1989 | | | | 1990 | | |
| --- | --- | --- | --- | --- | --- | --- | --- | --- | --- |
| | Jul | Oct | Jan | Apr | Jul | Oct | Jan | Apr | Jun |
| **Experimental estate** | | | | | | | | | |
| Rubbish | 14 | 17 | 17 | 15 | 16 | 17 | 13 | 13 | 14 |
| Graffiti | 18 | 19 | 16 | 16 | 14 | 16 | 16 | 17 | 18 |
| Property damage | 8 | 9 | 12 | 9 | 11 | 13 | 10 | 10 | 11 |
| Paths and fences | 8 | 15 | 12 | 11 | 13 | 15 | 13 | 7 | 9 |
| AVERAGE | 12 | 15 | 14 | 13 | 13 | 15 | 13 | 12 | 13 |
| **Control estate** | | | | | | | | | |
| Rubbish | 19 | 23 | 20 | 17 | 18 | 24 | 19 | 19 | 21 |
| Graffiti | 21 | 19 | 15 | 7 | 9 | 10 | 11 | 20 | 16 |
| Property damage | 10 | 9 | 11 | 8 | 16 | 16 | 19 | 18 | 16 |
| Paths and fences | 6 | 5 | 9 | 6 | 9 | 12 | 10 | 3 | 6 |
| AVERAGE | 14 | 14 | 14 | 10 | 13 | 15 | 15 | 15 | 15 |
| **Dodthorpe** | | | | | | | | | |
| Rubbish | 23 | 26 | 20 | 18 | 19 | 25 | 13 | 10 | 8 |
| Graffiti | 27 | 32 | 21 | 27 | 25 | 22 | 6 | 8 | 8 |
| Property damage | 0 | 5 | 2 | 2 | 0 | 2 | 0 | 0 | 0 |
| Paths and fences | 10 | 16 | 5 | 14 | 14 | 12 | 0 | 3 | 4 |
| AVERAGE | 15 | 20 | 12 | 15 | 14 | 15 | 5 | 5 | 5 |
| **Homethorpe** | | | | | | | | | |
| Rubbish | 6 | 6 | 8 | 7 | 5 | 10 | 9 | 9 | 9 |
| Graffiti | 9 | 10 | 9 | 11 | 9 | 14 | 27 | 28 | 30 |
| Property damage | 10 | 10 | 14 | 13 | 15 | 19 | 16 | 16 | 17 |
| AVERAGE | 7 | 7 | 8 | 8 | 8 | 11 | 14 | 14 | 14 |

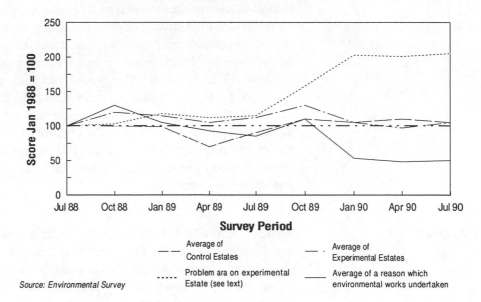

*Figure 9.4* **Environmental nuisance scores: Hull experimental and control estates compared**

Survey Period

Average of Control Estates

Average of Experimental Estates

Problem ara on experimental Estate (see text)

Average of a reason which environmental works undertaken

*Source: Environmental Survey*

9.23  Jenthorpe was in the midst of building work when the survey was conducted in June 1990 and the score there had risen. The Asthorpe flats, on which major environmental and security work was undertaken, showed no major change through the study period. These flats were well kept to start with. They already had entry phones as did all the blocks on the Thorpes before the project began. The addition of video cameras seems to have had no effect.

*Figure 9.5* **Environmental nuisance scores: Experimental estate in Hull area of completed works undertaken**

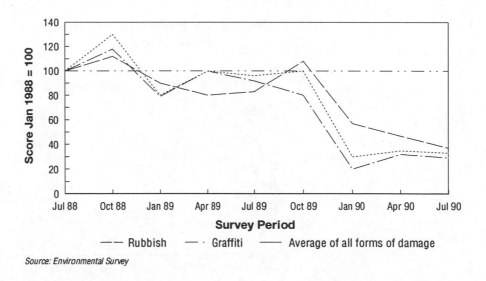

Survey Period

—— Rubbish    — · Graffiti    —— Average of all forms of damage

*Source: Environmental Survey*

9.24  The significant worsening took place in and around one block of flats. From mid 1989 these began to show marked worsening in rubbish and internal damage scores and a lesser increase in the graffiti levels. The average score rose from 6.6 in July 1988 to 14.0 in June 1990 with most of the rise occurring after the summer of 1989. Certainly building work began on the flats in November 1989 but the main factor seems to have been the changing social composition. It was the combined effect of the local authority's intention to keep families out of flats and a desire to increase the number of homeless and at risk people the authority would house.

9.25 The flats had always housed some formerly single homeless people (their first accommodation) but the numbers began to rise. Local managers had to find places for these new tenants in the one part of the estate where they had vacancies. With a small but growing group of more demanding tenants giving rise to nuisances and damage, the caretaking service and informal social controls in the block seem to have become unable to cope or contain the situation. The situation deteriorated suddenly and sharply (see Figure 9.6). Once that happened tenants and caretakers alike gave up or lost heart. Conditions in the flats degenerated. A fire made one floor uninhabitable and serious damage to public areas lead to the closure of another whole floor. Our survey shows the effect spread beyond the flats to the surrounding areas. There was a proposal to introduce concierges into the blocks to ensure a continuous personal presence and oversight.

**Evaluation**

9.26 The results in Hull therefore confirm several of the original elements in the theory advanced by PEP. Physical improvements discussed in detail with the tenants, bringing greater privacy to the houses, does seem to have produced a marked improvement in the environment that has been sustained, at least over the year since the renovation to the first Thorpe was completed. Experience on the Danes, another part of the Orchard Park Estate, on which PEP had worked in a similar way several years ago, suggests an improved environment can be sustained. The experience also bears out PEP's warnings about the importance of the local authority allocations policy and the social mix on estates. An increase in the proportion of vulnerable people in even a small geographical area can make a decisive difference in and beyond the immediate living area. This suggests that extreme care must be exercised not to push blocks beyond that tipping point and that public authorities should accept that if the aim of policy is to house more vulnerable people in traditional housing, it has consequences for housing management, both its kind and intensity.

*Figure 9.6* **Environmental nuisance scores: Hull experimental estate - Block 6 flats**

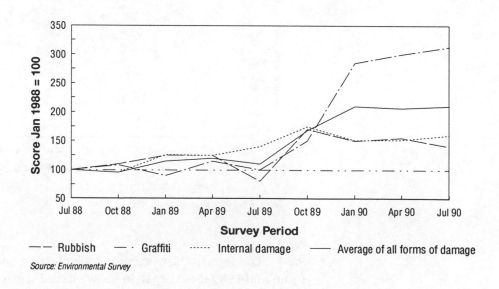

Source: Environmental Survey

9.27 The results also have mixed messages for the model with which we began. The improvements in crime on the control estate in London took place despite the fact that there had been no major improvement in "incivilities" or the appearance of the estate, except on one block. Underlying social change seemed to be the force at work. In Hull the positive outcomes of environmental change could be rapidly swamped by a change in social composition.

*Figure 9.7*   **Environmental nuisance scores: Hull control estate**

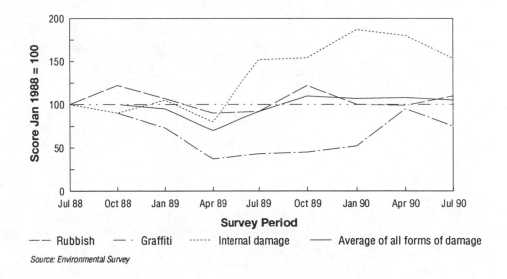

Source: Environmental Survey

# Chapter 10

The repairs function

**The PEP ideal**

10.1   The model espoused by PEP always gave repairs a central role. The PEP Guide put it this way :

> " *The origins of intensive housing management in the nineteenth century were founded on repairs as an integral part of a good landlord service and as the direct responsibility of the housing manager.*" *(p 6).*

PEP proposed:

(i)   The attachment of local repairs teams to the estate office with its own foreman responsible to the estate manager.

(ii)   A local estate based ordering facility so that tenants could go into their local estate office and make a repairs request.

(iii)   Local estate based progress chasing on that request.

10.2   A run down estate needed one repairs worker for every hundred dwellings. The estate office should be competent to receive and progress repairs. This involved being able to take the repairs request, order repairs, track, arrange for completions and billing or payment. Thus the PEP model has been based on a system of tenant initiated responsive repairs.

10.3   Since these original principles were set down the Government introduced the requirement that most local authority repairs work should be subject to regular compulsory tendering.

10.4   This made it more difficult to keep a permanent group of workers together on an estate who knew the estate.

10.5   Later PEP was to give more emphasis to planned maintenance. This involved making a regular survey of the estate, assessing the condition of the property, recording it, preparing a long term rolling programme of maintenance and a long term budget (Power and PEP 1991).

**Implementing the ideal**
The London
experimental estate
*A local repairs team*

10.6   For the first nine months of the research the estate was given a three man local repairs team allocated from the council's direct labour organisation (DLO). One was a plumber, one a carpenter and one was a chargehand who did no repairs himself. Larger jobs were ordered from four named private contractors or the central DLO.

10.7   Then in April 1988 this local DLO team was replaced by a private contractor who had won the Measured Term Contract which covered six of the eight local repairs teams in the Neighbourhood. The new repairs team covered two estates and in practice repairmen were moved around between the six estates. In November 1988 there were ten operatives working on the estate because the new team leader and the housing team were generating such a lot of work.

10.8　When the MTC was again put out to tender the following year the DSO won it back. Specific operatives were assigned to each estate but operatives were required to cover work in other parts of the Neighbourhood. The DSO was unable to do all the work generated and the estate office was permitted to use private contractors.

10.9　In 1990 the MTC was let on a three year basis and was again won by the DSO. For budgetary reasons the repairs and maintenance budget was cut in half.

*Local ordering*

10.10　The local ordering of repairs began with the creation of the housing team and the opening of the office on the estate allowed it to flourish. It was popular with tenants. However, initially the paper work was very unwieldy. Each repair was supposed to be entered **four** times and the information tended not to tally. Computerisation late in 1988 helped simplify the procedure.

*Local monitoring*

10.11　The checking of jobs to see whether the repairs team had fulfilled its contractual obligations was part of the housing team's new role. In theory it was to be undertaken on a percentage of the jobs ordered. In practice it was done in an **ad hoc** way. An investigation by the internal auditors in 1989 revealed that this required checking was not being done by most offices in the Neighbourhood. Only then did the team formalise the process.

*Assessment*

10.12　It is clear from this brief history that nothing like the PEP ideal was ever achieved in the case of the London estate. Local job ordering for tenants was successful. So too was the local monitoring.

10.13　The repairs team element of the PEP model was only implemented for a year. The imperatives of the DSO were different to the PEP model. They had to make a minimum return on capital invested and thought that was inconsistent with the small teams PEP advocated. The result of putting the function out to tender on an annual basis was to break any continuity between the local office and the repairs team.

The London control
estate

*Repairs team*

10.14　The picture on the control estate was not that different. In the first year the housing staff could go to the central DSO or a private contractor depending on which was able to do the work. In the second year a local DSO team of 7 was set up to cover an area comprising 1,200 properties, 2 to 3 times the size of the experimental estate. The foreman had daily, if not twice daily, contact with the office staff although the repairs team were based out on one of the estates. On the whole relations worked well. The housing team continued to be able to use named private contractors though two of them proved unusable for different reasons. In the third year, the DSO again won the contract, but moved it operatives around more flexibly between estates than before. As on the experimental estate, they were unable to undertake all jobs and in the beginning of 1990 the housing team was able once again to go to private contractors for work the DSO could not undertake. Because of underspending elsewhere in the Neighbourhood the team managed to spend around 70% more than its budget!

10.15　In 1990, a three year contract was made with the DSO to provide repairs and maintenance services as on the experimental estate. While the repairs budget had not been cut to the same extent, worries existed here too that the DSO would not be able to undertake all the work needed.

10.16 Because there was no estate based office, repairs ordering was less local than on the experimental estate. Many repairs were requested on the phone. No computer ordering of jobs was available and the paper work continued to be hard to manage because of the quantities of repairs ordered.

*Monitoring*

10.17 More regular checking of actual repairs was undertaken by this office than the experimental office, partly because there was an unqualified surveyor working as a technical officer, part of whose job it was to undertake such work. A system where tenants signed for jobs completed was instigated, as it was for a time on the experimental estate, but it was not particularly successful as it depended on the operative returning the completed slip to the office. Those returned were largely illegible.

*The results*

10.18 The main performance indicator we chose to test the impact of the different repairs systems was the completion times of all the jobs raised during the period of study.

10.19 Not all jobs need to be completed immediately and to run a successful maintenance and repair business, longer term work needs to be stacked ready to fill the troughs of work in a system which is based on response to demand. Thus, asking if all jobs have been undertaken within three weeks, does not give a complete picture. However, with an efficient organisation, a good proportion of repairs ordered should be completed within that time scale. Because of the problems at the start of the research in even obtaining accurate figures for the numbers of jobs ordered (all the sources in Tower Hamlets differed on this) no attempt was made to record whether the job was undertaken within the time specified but simply how long it took for each job to be done. Once repairs ordering was computerised it was much easier to record the figures but it was decided to continue with the system forced on us by the manual systems in Hull so there would be a comparison.

10.20 The results do show substantial changes at times when the systems of management changed and suggest that the trends reflect real impacts even if the precise percentages should be treated with caution (see Table 10.1).

*Table 10.1* **Repairs completion times - experimental estate (Tower Hamlets) (percentages)**

|  | Within 1 week | 1-4 weeks | 4-12 weeks | Over 12 weeks | Incomplete cancelled |
|---|---|---|---|---|---|
| July 1987 | 14 | 45 | 38 | 3 | - |
| January 1988 | 42 | 14 | 3 | 1 | 40 |
| April 1988 | 61 | 17 | 4 | 2 | 16 |
| July 1988 | 50 | 24 | 9 | 2 | 15 |
| October 1988 | 63 | 12 | 8 | 1 | 13 |
| January 1989 | 58 | 24 | 4 | 2 | 12 |
| April 1989 | 58 | 17 | 6 | 1 | 18 |
| July 1989 | 38 | 29 | 3 | 4 | 26 |
| October 1989 | STRIKE |  |  |  |  |
| January 1990 | 48 | 7 |  |  | 45 |
| April 1990 | 49 | 18 | 6 | 4 | 23 |

10.21 When the research began only 14% of repairs on the experimental estate were being completed within a week of being requested, 45% were taking up to a **month** and 38% were taking from **four** to **twelve** weeks. The local team was then appointed and began work. By January 1988 over 40% of the jobs were being completed within a week and a large backlog of jobs had been cleared off the books or cancelled. By April of the next year after the new local estate team had been at work for about six months the number of repairs completed in one week had risen to 60%. This was the time when private contractors were appointed to do the same job. The immediate performance level falls but as they got used to the job it rose to a figure similar to that of the previous team. Performance remains at about the same level for the next year. It was at this point that the local team was broken up and the DSO took over again. Performance plummets so that only 38% of the repairs are completed in a week. The next period is confused by a strike and no useful statistics could be collected as jobs were not being accepted. Performance improves again in 1990 but not to the level then held when a local team was involved.

*Table 10.2* **Repairs completion times - control estate (Tower Hamlets) (percentages)**

|  | Within 1 week | 1-4 weeks | 4-12 weeks | Over 12 weeks | Incomplete cancelled |
|---|---|---|---|---|---|
| July 1987 |  |  |  |  |  |
| October 1987 |  |  |  |  |  |
| Janaury 1988* | ~36 | 30 | 16 | 2 | 16 |
| April 1988* | ~24 | 48 | 13 | - | 15 |
| July 1988* | ~50 | 24 | 8 | 4 | 17 |
| October 1988* | ~63 | 18 | 8 | - | 12 |
| January 1989* | 52 | 19 | 9 | 2 | 18 |
| April 1989* | 55 | 21 | 8 | 5 | 11 |
| July 1989* | 50 | 16 | 7 | 5 | 22 |
| October 1989* | 52 | 19 | 7 | - | 22 |
| January 1990* | 51 | 10 | 6 | 1 | 31 |
| April 1990* | 45 | 24 | 10 | 1 | 21 |
| June 1990* | 47 | 21 | 10 | 1 | 22 |

\* DLO figure only
~ from incomplete figures

10.22 For the control estate complete statistics are only available from the DSO and even then not for all periods. However, at only one point do the performance levels reach those of the experimental estate, in October 1988 (see Table 10.2). Moreover, the distinct improvement that takes place, does so immediately after the DSO is decentralised to a local, if not an estate, base (the figures for July 1988 and subsequently).

Evaluation

10.23 Despite the imperfect implementation of the estate based ideal, these results do confirm the hypothesis that devolution of the repairs function to the estate office increases response effectiveness. Less decisive devolution can also produce results but not as dramatic.

10.24 Another indicator of change is the impact of the local office and local ordering on the frequency with which tenants ask for repairs to be done. We saw that there were difficulties in the operation of the local team on the experimental estate early on. The local housing office had always been reasonably close for tenants who wished to report repairs so the local office was less significant than we shall see in Hull. The control estate was extremely good at getting its repairs budget spent and thus, towards the end of the financial year was likely to get unspent balances from other offices to spend. Taken together these factors probably explain why the differences between the control and experimental estates are not consistent as far as demand for repairs is concerned (see Table 10.3).

*Table 10.3* **Repairs ordered by month 1987-90 on experimental and control estate in Tower Hamlets**

|  | Experimental estate | Control estate |
| --- | --- | --- |
| July 1987 | 112 | NA |
| October 1987 | NA | 150 (incomplete DLO figures) |
| January 1988 | 188 | 165 |
| April 1988 | 100 | 91 |
| July 1988 | 132 | 194 |
| October 1988 | 157 | 215 |
| January 1989 | 207 | 259 |
| April 1989 | 155 | 135 |
| July 1989 | 118 | 212 |
| October 1989 | 87 (Strike) | 123 (Strike) |
| January 1990 | 199 | 190 |
| April 1990 | 151 | 281 |

10.25    One of the expected but positive results of having a local estate team was that for the first time a group of housing officers identified with the estate and began to notice not only major dilapidation but also a pattern in the repairs requested by tenants. One example of this was the flow of complaints about the drains on one of the older blocks on the experimental estate. The manager initiated further investigation and found that the main drainage system was in need of major repairs and upgrading. This was put into the capital programme.

**Implementation in Hull**
The experimental estate
*A local repairs team*

10.26    In April 1988 a local repairs team was set up using DSO staff to cover the two neighbouring PEP estates. The chargehand went to the PEP team training. The team was 15 strong covering most trades.

10.27    The team was responsible for 2,000 properties in all. This was slightly less than the one in a hundred properties norm PEP had originally proposed but when work overloaded them they could draw on the central DSO and when work was slack they were asked to help out with work for the central DSO. This gave a flexibility and economic use of the manpower. The chargehand who set up the team was particularly successful in producing an effective unit.

*Repairs ordering*

10.28    Repairs had been ordered through a repairs reporting system based in the Hull central housing department. In April 1988, repairs for the experimental estate could be ordered through the neighbouring PEP estate office, and from September 1988 in the experimental office itself. Repairs ordered were put on to a central computer link in the office, but copies of orders were handed in person to the chargehand. (Previously, housing management staff had no links with the works depots.) It was up to the chargehand to order his priorities. To avoid the problems of "lost" repairs tickets, he instituted a system of signing for each repair handed over. Invoicing and monitoring was done on another computer in the office which was linked only to the neighbouring PEP estate. Some checking of jobs was undertaken by surveyors but the team leader was aware that he was signing invoices for payment for jobs done without much idea of whether they were well done or not. The DSO was paid the rate for the repair as it was ordered (emergencies, for instance, are paid at a higher rate) without any notice taken whether the job was done or not.

10.29   In April 1990 the experimental office took on the new computer system for repairs ordering and also the new post inspection procedures which had already been adopted on the control estate (see below). However, it kept its local repairs team, now provided by a private contractor. The lack of proper control and monitoring of the repairs function was made good.

10.30   Thus, in Hull, on the experimental site, the arrangements were close to the PEP ideal with both a local team and local requesting of repairs by tenants. However, there was no proper checking of the results.

The Hull control estate

10.31   When the research began, repairs on the control estate, like that in the rest of Hull, were organised on a traditional centralised pattern. Repairs were undertaken from an area base covering 9,000 properties but the area office housing staff were not supposed to contact the repairs depot directly. In the case of emergencies they actually did. Job ordering was undertaken through an office in central Hull which tenants contacted by card or phone. The area housing office had no internal telephone link to the repairs reporting team and faced the same problems as tenants in getting through to them on busy lines. What was recognised to be a poor and slow service was reorganised in October 1989 when a more localised system of ordering began and tenants could request repairs at any one of three housing offices on the whole estate. The DSO, however, was moving in the opposite direction and in April 1990 pulled more men off its local depot and controlled them centrally. Any queries about work were directed by the local housing office to the central DSO not the local depot.

10.32   The important change on the control estate was the monitoring and control of work. Some surveyors were put into the Area office and used the new Hull created computer programme and the detailed information it offered to pay the DSO by results. The result was a steep rise in cancellations as it paid the DSO to cancel a job rather than be penalised for doing it late. The Neighbourhood Management Assistants had been regraded and post inspections of repairs was added to their job descriptions. Hull's own housing management decentralisation programme concentrated on the role of monitoring of repairs using computers and checks and did not bother with the PEP approach of local liaison with a known repairs team to obtain a satisfactory repairs service.

The results

10.33   The most immediate result of localising the ordering on an estate base, was to double the number of repairs requests over night. The early figures exclude work on emergencies and voids on both estates. When they are included after April 1988 the total requests on the control estate rise by just under half. Local ordering on the experimental estate began at the same time and the number of orders rose there by two and a half times (see Table 10.4). That was what PEP's experience had been elsewhere.

10.34   Finding that their repairs requests were taken up and completed, as we shall see, tenants' requests went on rising, only showing some sign of stabilising in the last part of the research period. The level of repairs ordered was about four times as great at the end of the period as it was just before local ordering began, taking emergencies into account. The rise is less dramatic if an earlier base line is used, but on any measure a very significant change occurred. The local team was able to process and complete a much larger number of repairs in a shorter time. Precisely the same kind of result occurred when the control estate decentralised. Between July and October 1989 the number of orders more than doubled. Though they should have been warned by previous PEP estate experience, the council appears to have been taken by surprise. Demand for repairs has not gone on rising at the same rate for as long as on the experimental estate. In both cases the traditional rationing device of chocking off demand by making access to services difficult was given up and the consequences are clear. Better services create their own demand.

*Table 10.4*  **Repairs ordered by month 1987-90 on experimental and control estate in Hull**

|  | Experimental estate | Control estate |
|---|:---:|:---:|
| July 1987 | 211# | 162# |
| October 1987 | 176# | 111# |
| January 1988 | 99# | 110# |
| April 1988 | 253 | 160 |
| July 1988 | 311 | 186 |
| October 1988 | 397 | 238 |
| January 1989 | 381 | 203 |
| April 1989 | 403 | 205 |
| July 1989 | 286 | 144 |
| October 1989 | 431 | 357 |
| January 1990 | 591 | 436 |
| April 1990 | 580 | 299 |

\#  excludes emergencies and voids

10.35   In Hull, one of the managers reported that repairs requests to the central repairs reporting service had also increased although the service was only waiting to be decentralised.

10.36   To order repairs is one thing. To succeed in getting them done is another. Here, too, the local repairs team made a major difference. Again emergencies were excluded from the early figures. The control estate completion times suggest that this does affect the picture from January to April 1988 but by nothing like the effect of introducing the local repairs team on the experimental estate. The number of repairs completed in one week rises from less than 10% to 40% and then reaches 70% in April 1989 (see Table 10.5).

10.37   A high level of early completions was sustained until April 1990 when the contract was awarded to a private contractor who had never done such work. Penalties for non-completion in the allotted time were also introduced and that led to a large number of jobs being cancelled, as it had done on the control estate in the previous October. The introduction of the local monitoring and checking on the work of the largely centralised repairs service on the control estate also speeded up the repairs process (see Table 10.6).

*Table 10.5* **Repairs completion times - experimental estate (Hull) (percentages)**

|  | Within 1 week | 1-4 weeks | 4-12 weeks | Over 12 weeks | Incomplete cancelled |
|---|---|---|---|---|---|
| July 1987* | 12 | 47 | 25 | 7 | 9 |
| October 1987* | 2 | 9 | 56 | 21 | 12 |
| January 1988* | 6 | 30 | 40 | 3 | 10 |
| April 1988 | 38 | 38 | 20 | 2 | 2 |
| July 1988 | 47 | 39 | 11 | 1 | 1 |
| October 1988 | 51 | 26 | 19 | 3 | 1 |
| January 1989 | 62 | 25 | 7 | 1 | 5 |
| April 1989 | 71 | 13 | 10 | 1 | 4 |
| July 1989 | 63 | 18 | 15 |  | 4 |
| October 1989 | 62 | 22 | 10 | 3 | 3 |
| January 1990 | 57 | 24 | 12 | 4 | 3 |
| April 1990 | 38 | 19 | 6 |  | 37 |

\* figure does not include emergencies or voids

*Table 10.6* **Repairs completion times - control estate (Hull) (percentages)**

|  | Within 1 week | 1-4 weeks | 4-12 weeks | Over 12 weeks | Incomplete cancelled |
|---|---|---|---|---|---|
| July 1987* | 6 | 33 | 34 | 17 | 10 |
| October 1987* | 5 | 31 | 54 | 2 | 7 |
| January 1988* | 4 | 46 | 40 | 1 | 8 |
| April 1988 | 8 | 36 | 36 | 12 | 8 |
| July 1988 | 27 | 30 | 30 | 10 | 3 |
| October 1988 | 19 | 36 | 30 | 9 | 6 |
| January 1989 | 37 | 33 | 19 |  | 11 |
| April 1989 | 24 | 33 | 28 | 5 | 10 |
| July 1989 | 16 | 52 | 21 | 8 | 3 |
| October 1989 | 17 | 16 | 32 | 6 | 29 |
| January 1990 | 45 | 12 | 22 |  | 21 |
| April 1990 | 42 | 25 | 5 |  | 28 |

\* figure does not include emergencies or voids

**Planned maintenance**

10.38   Since the PEP guide was first written, PEP thinking has shifted from the responsiveness of the repairs team to repairs requests, to a greater emphasis on planned maintenance, which allows more rational use of operatives undertaking a programme of work rather than one-off jobs. It also reduces the need for responsive repairs.

10.39   This emphasis has been taken up in the London PEP Neighbourhood but it has been overtaken by events. A sum of money for planned maintenance was set aside in 1989/90. With the halving of the budget available, in Tower Hamlets planned maintenance has had to be forgotten.

10.40   In Hull, planned maintenance has always been a part of the programme of work. The need for the extension of the eaves on the roofs and window replacements on the experimental estate was identified under this programme.

The problem in Hull is that the pre-war and 1950s estates need upgrading but the ones built in the 1960s and 1970s are also in need of major repair because of the way they were built. A programme on the control estate similar to that on the experimental estate, but including increased insulation for the properties, seemed unlikely to get funded in the near future because of the needs of the many older properties in Hull.

**Conclusions**
Local ordering

10.41 Local ordering of jobs was very successful in both experimental estates. Clearly tenants were happy with this service and used it. More jobs were ordered on the experimental estates with estate based offices than on the controls, where repairs ordering was localised but not to estate level.

Local repairs teams

10.42 The local repairs teams were shown to be very effective at getting work done quickly. The local management of a local repairs service meant that the local housing offices were able to arrange access to property for the works operatives and were able to talk directly with the foreman or the workmen themselves about problems and complaints brought in by tenants. Obtaining repair work and organising it was helped greatly by everyone being on the same site. The second team leader on the experimental estate in London complained because the repairs team was housed elsewhere on the estate and was not in the same building as the housing management team.

Other changes affecting the service

10.43 Over the study period, the management of the repairs services improved on all the estates and this was due in part to legislative change and in part to the effects of decentralisation. The lack of proper controls over the work of the repairs team was shown in the way that, at the start of the research, payment was made automatically to the DSO, in London rather than being made on completion of a job. In Hull, the DSO was paid at the rate at which a job was ordered regardless of whether the job was undertaken within the time specified or not. Because of this there was no particular need to cancel jobs and so a backlog developed in both London and Hull of jobs which had been done and had not been invoiced or were actually not going to be done for one reason or another. In October 1989, in Hull, when payment became dependent on work being done within the specified time, the number of jobs cancelled increased dramatically thus reducing the backlog. The idea that each reported order represents a contract with the repairs body began to inform the housing management attitude on all the estates.

10.44 The financial consequences of running an efficient repairs ordering service were beginning to affect all the study areas by the end of the research period. An effective method of ordering and an efficient repairs organisation means that more jobs are undertaken. While they may cost less per job ordered than previously, overall there is an increase in the budget required. When that increase was felt only on the two PEP estates in Hull, the overall Hull housing budget was not deeply affected and the teams overspent in 1989/90 with impunity.

10.45 In Tower Hamlets the crisis was more advanced. Because of new regulations about the repayment of housing debt and the ring fencing of the Housing Revenue Account, less money was available in 1990/91. In Tower Hamlets some staff felt the experimental office was too available to tenants who could abuse their access to the office and continually ask for upgradings of their property. The Neighbourhood housing management, however, took the view that they needed to make a policy decision about which repairs should take priority, rather than using lack of access to the repairs service as a means of limiting its use and therefore the budget.

10.46    Annual tendering for work contracts caused problems. In both experimental sites, the changeover time was a difficult period as the new repairs team sorted out what it had to do and housing staff adjusted to working with a new repairs team. In Tower Hamlets there were three changes of team during the research period. Annual tendering is less appropriate where system built structures demand the accumulation of special knowledge and special repairs stocks. The move to a three year tendering period allowed for a more settled system to develop.

10.47    For the DSO, the decentralisation of housing management and repairs in Tower Hamlets posed a problem. The DSO managers were critical of the small size of the repairs teams set up by PEP. But whatever size of team they created during the study period, it was never right. Although they complained the estate offices did not provide enough work for a team to be viable, at the same time they were unable to do all the work ordered. Because they won the contract in two of the three years, the disorganisation they exhibited had a negative effect on the ability of the housing officers to produce a good repairs service. Tenants usually blamed housing staff when work was not done. While sometimes they had failed to order repairs, more often the repairs team had failed. A poorly managed repairs service increased the workload of the office staff.

10.48    The DSO found it hard to compete with small contractors because of their overheads and the employment conditions they offered their work force. There were high absentee and sickness rates, and low productivity.

**In brief**

10.49    In Hull especially, a local repairs team and local ordering, as advocated by PEP, did come into being and proved more responsive than the previous system. The local ordering introduced in the London experimental estate also increased demands. When Hull decentralised its other ordering functions in other offices the same thing occurred. The "centralised" system may have been effective in deterring demand but not in being responsive.

# Chapter 11

The allocation and lettings function

11.1   If an estate is unpopular the lettings function becomes crucial. Empty properties on an estate are a sure indication to the outsider that something is wrong and for those on the estate it is a depressing reminder that, in a world of housing shortage, people would rather not live on the estate. Vandalism breeds on vacant property so PEP has always put the capacity to let property high on its agenda. For the local authority, empty property means loss of income and higher rents for those housed.

**The PEP ideal**

11.2   PEP argued that highly centralised allocations and lettings procedures simply led to property standing empty for unnecessarily long periods. If prospective tenants could be identified quickly, shown vacant property at once, and the whole business of letting done on the spot, delays could be cut to a minimum. Thus, a local list of applicants, local administration procedures for signing up tenants and a recognised priority system were key elements in the PEP local lettings model. Speed of letting often also depended on necessary repairs being undertaken to make the property habitable and that, too, should be in the hands of the local team.

11.3   Local lettings did not mean that the authority's priority needs were ignored. Points schemes or other rationing procedures could be applied locally and monitored.

**Implementation in Tower Hamlets**
Experimental and control estates

11.4   Neither Tower Hamlets estate was the first choice of top priority applicants but neither estate could be described as really hard to let either. Tenants are usually realistic about their chances of being housed and will accept what they would not choose.

11.5   Allocations on the experimental and control estates in London were undertaken at Neighbourhood level. The local office staff did all other work on letting property. They contacted tenants and showed them round and signed them up. They were also responsible for dealing with empty property. Tenant turnover was one third higher on the experimental than on the control estate so the staff in the former office had more work.

11.6   At the beginning of the research period on the experimental estate there was talk of moving the computerised allocations work to the local offices following the PEP model. Staff opposed this. By the end of the period the site where allocations actually took place had become of small interest. The numbers of properties available to let had diminished for various reasons: right to buy sales, the homeless families quota allocated to each Neighbourhood, the abandonment of inter-Neighbourhood transfers, and the efficiency of the decentralised system which meant there was no longer a pool of unlet property as there had been at the start of the research.

11.7   Although neither experimental nor control office fulfilled the PEP ideal, there were few complaints about Neighbourhood level allocations. Those there were reflected local managers' desire to control all the services available to tenants. The fact they had to ask the Neighbourhood allocations officer for permission to transfer tenants within the estate was a minor annoyance. We observed estate officers in the unsatisfactory position of go-between between the allocations officers and prospective tenants. At the end of the research period, as so little property was available to let, an advice role on other housing possibilities was to be added to the allocations officers' work in the new local office for the experimental estate.

**The results**
Empty properties

11.8   Empty properties - "voids" in the ugly jargon of the housing manager's world - had been a major problem on the experimental estate but from 1986, housing officers had started to identify them. Void properties known to the local authority peaked at over 8% of all dwellings in February 1987, the month the housing team was established. The team made voids their first priority. This involved collecting information on all the voids, pushing the repairs work along and processing potential tenants as quickly as possible. By July 1987, at the start of the research, the team, although still not estate based, had succeeded in pushing down the voids rate - the percentage of empty property - to 6% and they reduced it steadily thereafter. In June 1980 the void rate was 2.5% and it was only that high because of particular circumstances. The team knew exactly what property was empty and the stage it was at in the process of reletting. This would not have been the case in 1985.

11.9   The eight outstanding empty properties on the estate at the end of the research period illustrate the problems the local team has to cope with. Four flats needed major works undertaken before they could be occupied, one had squatters in and the officers were waiting for a court order to remove the squatters. Another was an old persons dwelling that was proving very difficult to let.

11.10   A similar reduction in voids occurred on the control estate. The initial rise and then fall in known voids on the control estate happened a year later than on the experimental estate and it is likely that this was caused by the local team starting there a year later. The team on the control estate had to deal with widespread squatting, a situation which they had inherited, although a start had been made by housing officers in 1987 and early 1988 to solve this problem. By June 1990 the void rate was a very respectable 1.8% (see Table 11.1).

*Table 11.1*   **Void rates**

|  | Tower Hamlets | | Hull | |
| --- | --- | --- | --- | --- |
|  | Experimental | Control | Experimental | Control |
| January 1987 | 8.1 | | | |
| July 1987 | 6.2 | 4.0 | 3.3 | 1.1 |
| October 1987 | 3.2 | 4.9 | 3.6 | 1.5 |
| January 1988 | 3.4 | 6.1 | 3.4 | 1.2 |
| April 1988 | 3.4 | 5.9 | 2.8 | 1.8 |
| July 1988 | 4.1 | 3.7 | 3.6 | 2.6 |
| October 1988 | 3.4 | 2.4 | 3.6 | 1.8 |
| January 1989 | 2.6 | 3.0 | 3.4 | 1.9 |
| April 1989 | 3.0 | 3.8 | 4.2 | 1.9 |
| July 1989 | 2.8 | 2.4 | 5.5 | 1.7 |
| October 1989 | 2.0 | 2.2 | 4.3 | 2.1 |
| January 1990 | 3.2 | 1.4 | 3.9 | 1.1 |
| April 1990 | 2.7 | 1.7 | 4.8 | 1.0 |
| June 1990 | 2.5 | 1.8 | 5.4 | 1.6 |

11.11   Lettings times vary quite considerably from month to month. Some of the very long letting times are in fact a tribute to the way the teams managed to get to grips with problem property (e.g. the fire damaged flats on the experimental estate) or long term squatting. The figures show faster letting on the experimental estate than on the control estate up to half way through the research period in December 1988. After that the teams achieved similar varied results (see Table 11.2).

*Table 11.2*   **Quarterly average relet intervals in weeks**

|  | Tower Hamlets | | Hull | |
|---|---|---|---|---|
|  | Experimental | Control | Experimental | Control |
| **1987** | | | | |
| 3rd quarter | 23 | 40 | 9 | 6 |
| 4th quarter | 15 | 22 | 10 | 8 |
| **1988** | | | | |
| 1st quarter | 13 | 30 | 12 | 10 |
| 2nd quarter | 9 | 29 | 13 | 10 |
| 3rd quarter | 17 | 37 | 10 | 9 |
| 4th quarter | 14 | 22 | 13 | 11 |
| **1989** | | | | |
| 1st quarter | 10 | 14 | 14 | 10 |
| 2nd quarter | 11 | 23 | 13 | 9 |
| 3rd quarter | 151# | 30 | 13 | 8 |
| 4th quarter | 13 | 22 | 14 | 8 |
| **1990** | | | | |
| 1st quarter | 13 | 19 | 13 | 8 |
| 2nd quarter | 18 | 19 | 12 | 5 |

\#   caused by fire damaged property

**Implementation in Hull**
Experimental and control estates

11.12   The situation in Hull was very different to that in London. The experimental estate had the most really hard to let property of any of the research estates. The blocks of flats were no longer let to families with children and the pool of prospective tenants was small. Unpopular property was allocated to high risk, high need groups on the Council's waiting list as we have seen.

11.13   The difficulties experienced in one of the blocks of flats when young single people moved there has already been discussed in Chapter Nine. A fire on one floor and the wrecking of another floor led to a rise in the void rate as both floors were closed. A policy decision was made not to let the flats unless the applicants appeared suitable and the tenants were to be involved in the selection. This lengthened the letting time.

11.14   The control estate, by contrast, did not have high blocks of flats though there are four small grouped flats with a common entrance scattered among the houses. These also cause most of the management problems on this estate but nothing like those on the experimental estate.

11.15   Once again the local office had to work to a very clear central set of priorities in allocating housing units. The team made allocations from a computerised register covering the whole of Hull. They then showed the potential tenant round and made the letting as in London.

11.16    The Neighbourhood Housing Assistants (NHAs) undertook allocation work which on the control estate and elsewhere in Hull was undertaken by specialist allocators in the Area offices. On the control estate the tenant would simply be offered the key (there was no squatting problem) and would view the property alone. Work with homeless families was not undertaken in either office for it remained a centralised function. (Allocations had been decentralised in 1986 to the Area offices.)

## The results
### Empty properties

11.17    The experience of both the experimental and control estates shows that the localisation of voids control and lettings had a positive effect, in the one case by localisation to an estate base, in the other to a neighbourhood level.

11.18    An experienced local team began working on voids out of the neighbouring PEP office before the estate office opened. Although the team that set up that office finally was less experienced than the original team, the void rate did not start to rise above 4% until April 1989. On average over the three years it was 4.0%. It peaked in July 1989 at 5.5%. The team was not keeping up with the rising numbers of voids especially in the flats. One reason they gave for this was that on the neighbouring PEP estate the capital and security works on the blocks of flats had been completed and so, if offered a choice, prospective tenants were tending to opt for the improved block. The innovative scheme to furnish some flats to let to young at risk people was reasonably successful. Unfortunately, one bad case, where a flat was wrecked, did not help the image of the scheme or the void rate.

11.19    From the peak in July 1989, the team started slowly to reduce the voids again. But the fire and the damage to the public area of one floor started to drive the void level up again. The decision to take the flats out of the mainstream allocations procedure and not to let to very young people pushed the void rate back up to 5.5% at the end of the research period.

11.20    In contrast the control estate had nothing like the level of turnover of tenants on the experimental estate. The void rate started at 1.1% and remained by far the best of the research estates. Thus it peaked at 3% in September 1988. The lowest void rate - 1% in March 1990 - was recorded after the control estates' own decentralisation. The average void rate over the three year research period was 1.6%.

11.21    The other main aim of the localised allocations procedure was to speed the time it took to let property. A factor that affected the letting times on the Hull experimental estate was the very high turnover rate - 17% of tenants (especially from the flats) -compared with 11% on the control estate. From April 1989 to April 1990 on the experimental estate two officers, whose primary duty was rent arrears work, let on average 15 properties per month compared with the 7.5 let by specialist allocators on the control estate (and an average of about 3 on the London research estates). Letting intervals on the experimental estate rose from an average of 9 weeks in the first six months of the research (when the void rate was around 3.4) to under 13 weeks in the last six months (when the void rate was around 4.7). On the control estate comparable figures were 7 weeks (void rate 1.4) to 6.5 weeks (void rate 1.3).

11.22    The sheer number of voids on the experimental estate put pressure on other services i.e. surveyors, repairs teams. The housing management team's role in pushing them to act speedily on void property was not as developed as it became with localisation on the control estate.

**In brief**

11.23
- It is difficult to draw conclusions from a simple comparison of figures on the experimental and control estates either in Hull or London.

- The devolved responsibility for voids to local management does seem to have been important in both the control and experimental sites in London. The greater speed of letting on the experimental estate in Tower Hamlets might be put down to the team's physical presence on the estate which acted to remind staff of voids.

- In Hull, on the experimental estate voids rose. Estate based management **per se** did not reduce them. Procedures of letting did not change and were not different on the control and experimental estates except that there were no specialist lettings officers on the experimental estate. The fact that voids did not rise on the control estate is probably due to the lack of very unpopular flats.

- The key issue in Hull was the allocations policy. While it was an open and fair policy that people could see and understand, it led unintentionally to the placing of a lot of vulnerable single people in the blocks of flats. Taking the flats out of the usual allocations procedures and including current tenants in the selection of new tenants helped calm the situation down.

- It can be argued that in Hull Orchard Park was, at the beginning of the research period, on the edge of social collapse of the kind seen in some of the very worst estates. The fragile nature of the social situation is well illustrated by the events described. They illustrate the importance of allocations policy and local knowledge.

# Chapter 12      Rent collection and arrears

**The PEP ideal**

12.1   For PEP the local administration of rent collection and reducing arrears was one of the most important elements of estate based management. The move to distanced Giro or banking arrangements for rent collection had been disastrous for the personal presence of the housing department on estates. Door to door rent collection had long gone but it had meant that tenants were seen regularly and that there was early warning about arrears with the possibility of giving personal guidance or assistance in special cases.

12.2   In the modern situation the impersonal local council was likely to come second to the present and insistent hire purchase salesman or debt collector and the immediate sanction of having one's electricity or gas cut off. The alternative to a door to door rent collection service was for the local office to take on the collection and arrears chasing function. It would be the local office staff who would visit immediately a tenant fell into arrears and seek to find out why and whether there had been an error or whether help was needed. It also showed that the local office was not going to forget or ignore the fact. Even so, on an estate that is the last resort, officers will find it difficult to enforce the sanction of eviction for, under the homeless legislation families at risk are likely to reappear with no other housing option. Unfortunately, despite the importance PEP attached to estate based rent collection and arrears control, it was not implemented on either of the control estates in this study for reasons we describe below.

**Implementing the ideal**
The London
experimental estate

12.3   In Tower Hamlets rent was supposed to be paid by Giro at a Post Office. Arrears control was carried out at neighbourhood level and the estate based team was not involved at all. The local authority senior management wanted to decentralise arrears and rent collection to the estate office but the local staff were resistant. The arrears officers in the neighbourhood office argued that this was a specialist function that could not be devolved efficiently. PEP had convinced the local authority but the local authority had been unable to implement its intention. As it happened there was a pilot experiment of another kind in progress, the piloting of a move to administer housing benefit from the estate office. The housing benefit officer was able to deal with many of the rent queries that came into the office, so fortuitously the local contact was not entirely absent. However, this pilot scheme did not lead to the housing benefit function being decentralised to the local office. It remained a neighbourhood function because of staff opposition to the move.

12.4   The most significant change to occur during the period of the research had nothing to do with the experiment. It was the change in Government housing benefit policy that required all tenants to pay part of their rate bill regardless of income instead of some being exempt altogether. It was meant to bring home to tenants the effect of high rates set by some local authorities, in the Government's view. Whatever the merits of that argument, the direct result it had on all the estates was significantly to increase the levels of arrears. The results are evident from Table 12.1. Cumulative rent arrears expressed as a percentage of the annual net charge the local authority could expect to gather

from the estate, rose from 12.9% in October 1987 to 16.3 % in June 1990. At the same time the percentage of tenants actually in any arrears at all did not change greatly and indeed fell slightly from 61% to 56% (see Table 12.2). Overall arrears per tenant rose from £203 to £250 in the three years (see Table 12.3). It did, however, fall significantly from the end of 1988 when the administration of the local office improved.

*Table 12.1* **Cumulative rent arrears as a percentage of net annual charge**

|  | Tower Hamlets | | Hull | |
|  | Experimental | Control | Experimental | Control |
| --- | --- | --- | --- | --- |
| October (87-88) | 12.9 | # | 4.7 | 4.6 |
| March (87-88) | 14.0 | 10.8 | 5.3 | 5.7 |
| October (88-89) | 15.5 | 10.6 | 7.8 | 8.6 |
| March (88-89) | 14.6 | 13.5 | 9.2 | 11.2 |
| Oct/Nov (89-90) | 15.2 | 13.7 | 11.6 | 14.8 |
| March (89-90) | 12.3 | 14.1 | 13.0 | 15.1 |
| June (90-91) | 16.3 | 20.0 | 23.0 | 21.8 |

\# not available

*Table 12.2* **Percentage of tenants in arrears**

|  | Tower Hamlets | | Hull | |
|  | Experimental | Control | Experimental | Control |
| --- | --- | --- | --- | --- |
| **1987** | | | | |
| June/July | - | - | 34 | 37 |
| Oct/Nov | 61 | 51 | 35 | 38 |
| **1988** | | | | |
| Jan | 56 | 63 | 36 | 46 |
| April | 66 | 64 | 52 | 52 |
| July | 61 | 62 | 53 | 52 |
| Oct | 57 | 55 | 56 | 60 |
| **1989** | | | | |
| Jan | 52* (49) | 53 | 58 | 57 |
| April | 58* (55) | 57 | 55 | 57 |
| July | 54* (52) | 55 | 65 | 68 |
| Oct/Nov | 56 (53) | 62 | 61 | 61 |
| **1990** | | | | |
| Jan | 61 (64) | 70 | 61 | 63 |
| April | 57 (58) | 62 | 62 | 61 |
| June | 56 (56) | 59 | 59 | 60 |

\* Estimated
( ) Extended estate

**Table 12.3** **Average arrears per tenant in arrears (£s)**

|  | Tower Hamlets | | Hull | |
|  | Experimental | Control | Experimental | Control |
|---|---|---|---|---|
| **1987** | | | | |
| June/July | 203 | | 63 | 66 |
| Oct/Nov | | 173 | 71 | 68 |
| **1988** | | | | |
| Jan | 217 | 175 | 64 | 70 |
| April | 207 | 191 | 53 | 57 |
| July | 260 | 210 | 82 | 88 |
| Oct | 300 | 236 | 93 | 104 |
| **1989** | | | | |
| Jan | 314* (275) | 241 | 116 | 130 |
| April | 258* (225) | 227 | 142 | 164 |
| July | 278* (216) | 237 | 150 | 158 |
| Oct/Nov | 289 | 269 | 158 | 180 |
| **1990** | | | | |
| Jan | 238 (203) | 268 | 183 | 183 |
| April | 241 (203) | 294 | 182 | 187 |
| June | 250 (213) | 271 | 185 | 187 |

\* Estimated
( ) Extended estate

**The control estate**

12.5 Essentially the same system of rent arrears control existed on the control estate until April 1990 when this was devolved to the local team after a regrading exercise. Here, however, arrears rose sharply and continuously. The percentage of tenants in arrears rose and so did the average of arrears per tenant in arrears (see Tables 12.2. and 12.3).

12.6 Given that arrears control was not an estate based function in either experimental or control estates it is difficult to draw conclusions from these differences. However, it may be that the placing of housing benefit advice at estate level and the generally closer contact with tenants maintained in the estate office was part of the explanation of the better record on arrears on the experimental estate.

**The Hull experimental estate**

12.7 Rent was collected in the area office not the estate office. That office was sited in a run down shopping centre near the estate. Information on arrears was sent to the experimental estate office on a fortnightly basis. It took the form of a printout with all arrears listed. These were then taken on by the assistants in the estate office along with their other work. Arrears took about half the time of the staff concerned. The burden of that work rose for the same reasons as in London and because of computer problems in the central housing benefit computer section. The higher levels of unemployment and dependency on benefit help explain the more rapid rise in arrears in Hull, a five fold increase in the three years (see Table 12.1).

**The control estate**    12.8    Rent was collected in the Area office in the same way as the experimental estate and the arrears checks and follow ups were the same. The rise in cumulative arrears was very similar (see Table 12.1) as are the other indicators (see Tables 12.2 and 12.3).

**In brief**    12.9    The PEP model was not implemented. Moreover, extraneous factors seem to have had the major impact on rent collection. In addition to the changes in Housing Benefit, other local factors also operated. The effectiveness of the Housing Benefit sections was another critical factor. The largest arrears were often accounted for by the non payment of housing benefit by the council to itself. The right to buy also had an effect on the statistics because properties remained on the books even when they had been sold. The ex tenants were counted as in arrears even though as the new owners they were not supposed to be paying rent. The sale of council houses decreased the number of "good payers" and increased the proportion of poorer tenants.

12.10    However, the experimental estate in London did show a less steep rise in rent arrears and this may reflect the localised housing benefit advice and local contact with tenants sustained by the estate office.

# Chapter 13

Capital works

13.1    PEP argues that capital works are necessary on its estates because of the neglect that most hard to let estates have suffered. But the capital works to be undertaken must be linked closely to tenants' desires. The PEP guide quotes examples of capital works that have been undertaken without tenant consultation and the waste that has resulted leading to further cynicism about the Council from tenants. We came across an example where tenants were consulted on works but when they started two years later a furious tenants meeting rejected what the previous tenants had chosen and wanted to change the building programme. Because of the long lead time for most capital work and the fact that those that are consulted are often not those that benefit, PEP places more emphasis on tenant involvement in on-going management. Nevertheless, it is concerned that tenants should be consulted on capital works.

13.2    A large number of capital projects took place on three of the four research estates. There were only minor works on the control estate in Hull.

**Hull**

13.3    On the experimental estate in Hull about £5.5 million was to be spent. £1.5 million was allocated by Estate Action for planned maintenance to improve the weather resistance of the system built houses. £1.3 million was allocated to major environmental improvements. While the labour was funded from different training programmes, training staff and PEP coordinator's salaries as well as the cost of the materials came from the £1.3 million Estate Action allocations. The work was only about half finished by the end of the project.

13.4    The PEP coordinator took on a major role in the liaison and control of capital works and applications for funding. A team of architects was present on the estate for one year. Both architects and coordinator took part in tenant consultation as well as the housing team leader. They provided much more of the supervision and control of the works than was available to the housing team in Tower Hamlets, who were putting in applications and liaising over the works themselves and suffered a more distant relationship with the surveyors' department.

13.5    The work involved an extensive programme of alteration with the aim of making the environment more secure and giving people "defensible space" i.e. front gardens. Other security measures involved blocking off through walkways to make more private paths where an intruder could be recognised as such. Previously the estate was a warren of pathways.

13.6    The environmental changes also involved the removal of the pedestrian ways through the estate by increasing garden size where tenants wished. This removed public space from the estate thus cutting down the area that needed Council maintenance.

13.7    A further £1.5 million was allocated from Estate Action allocations to **planned maintenance**. Surveyors had identified a major problem in the system built houses: the eaves did not extend far enough and the walls became damp as they were not protected from rain. There were also severe problems of condensation and the houses were cold because "no-fines" construction did not provide enough insulation. The houses were expensive to heat with the underfloor electric heating provided. Also many window frames were beginning to rot. The eaves were extended, windows replaced, guttering and pipework replaced where necessary, the houses were painted both to improve their sombre appearance (different rows were painted different colours), and to improve insulation.

13.8   Many houses had had gas heating installed (this was a choice tenants had) and this programme continued. A heat exchanger system was tested during the research period and was found to be a successful method of reducing bills.

13.9   The block of flats already had door entry systems but these were often abused and frequently did not work. The doors were replaced and video cameras installed in the entrance halls and lifts. A viewing room allowed caretakers to check who had come in and out, although, as is often the case, there were technical problems. The ground floors of the blocks of flats were altered in some cases to make a tenants' room, taking away the underused and abused bicycle sheds. (However, the problem in Hull should not be overstated. The laundry rooms on the ground floor continued to be used for spinning of wet clothes and they have never become the derelict eyesores of laundries on the London estates.)

13.10   Outside, the areas round the flats were landscaped, pulling adjoining blocks into one unit and preventing the use of the ground floor of the blocks as passageways to other parts of the estate.

**Hull control estate**

13.11   The only works on the control estate involved the demolition of some vandalised and unused garages and the enclosure of the entrances of the sets of four flats which were subject to graffiti. Interestingly a lot of the doors on these entrances are left unlocked but they have on the whole proved a sufficient deterrent to vandalism.

**Tower Hamlets experimental estate**

13.12   On the desk access, seventies, system built blocks, a primary system of security and left replacement (funded through the Advanced Leasing programme) had already been agreed though it had not begun at the start of the research period. During the first year of the study, a secondary system of security was also proposed by the team leader. Additional funds were applied for from Estate Action by the acting team leader at the end of the first year for the conversion of a derelict laundry area into a training facility. The new team leader then proposed additions and changes to the proposed secondary security system. These changes were largely defined by her at a time when the tenant body was moribund.

13.13   The components of the £550,000 plus scheme funded from Estate Action allocations were porches on the block entrances; division of some decks by locking doors where tenants voted for this; public balcony grills; entrance gateways to the estate to give the area more privacy; works to secure garage areas; enclosure of garden areas around the ground floor flats; replacement of fire doors to each flat which were blocked up by many tenants because they were used as access by burglars. By the end of the research period many, though not all of these works were finished. A sub-contractor went out of business and the installed doors were unsuitable. So although the porches were proposed in the first year of the research they were still awaiting completion in June 1990. On the other hand, the conversion of the old laundry into a room for employment training schemes was mooted in September 1988, and was completed in early 1990.

13.14　A package of proposals for the system built part of the estate was put together by the acting team leader and the assistant Neighbourhood Housing Manager following consultation with tenants. This was presented along with proposals from other estate offices to the LDDC for funding. But the funding originally thought to be available through the LDDC never materialised. The second team leader did obtain some funds from the LDDC to help equip the training centre.

13.15　On the older part of the estate, window replacements (installation of UPVC window frames) had been started on some blocks and then left, giving an odd appearance. This work was completed in the first year. Central heating and door entry systems were installed over the research period in most blocks funded from the Advanced Leasing Programme. Enveloping works for one block (funded through HIP) were set up in the first year. But most of the other works were prepared and agreed after the first year. At the end of the research period, enveloping work on most of the blocks was either completed or under way. Environmental works were leading to the removal of eyesores such as unused washing line poles and the enhancement of courtyards.

13.16　The proposals were put forward by the housing team working with surveyors and landscape architects. It was difficult at the time to establish how far tenants were involved in the decisions. On some schemes, e.g. the training unit, tenants were not asked because of the pressure to get the application in quickly although they were informed it had gone in. The results of an early survey on tenants' views were never handed to the landscape architect working on the scheme.

**Tower Hamlets control estate**

13.17　The GLC had left money for improvements to the three tower blocks on the estate. The use of their money in this way across London was challenged in the courts. By the time the money was released it was worth less because of inflation. The housing team decided to concentrate on one block, the least abused, and really improve that rather than spreading the money thinly and achieving little. In 1989 allocations were agreed for the other two blocks. The entrance halls and vandalised ground and first floor public areas were completely changed to provide tenants' rooms and less vandalised public space. Entryphones were installed and lifts replaced. Some entrances to the blocks were removed. The first block was finished in 1989 and has continued largely unvandalised.

13.18　The underground garage area was leased in 1988 by News International for the use of its Wapping staff, although existing tenant garage users were able to continue using their spaces. The garages were given a coat of paint and security guards patrolled. An area that was derelict and unpleasant to enter felt safe once more.

13.19　Two of the other blocks benefitted from security works. Stairwells were improved, but despite entryphones and restricted access, the block that was worst for graffiti out of all the research estates, continued to suffer graffiti, though not to the previous extent. One neglected 1930s block mainly inhabited by Bengalis was improved by entryphones and a door system but it was 'patched up' rather than seriously upgraded. One series of deck access blocks with highly vandalised stairwells was improved with a coat of paint and strong glass, but even so continued to be vandalised.

**In brief**

13.20   In Hull a well prepared and thought out programme was slowly coming to fruition. The lack of provision of play facilities, seen to be a problem by tenants, was not addressed, but overall the improvements were popular.

13.21   The capital programme on the London experimental estate was not undertaken with tenant consultation in striking contrast to Hull.

13.22   Large sums of money were devoted to security works on the experimental estate without an analysis of the crime problem. The first application for Estate Action funding labelled the estate as very crime ridden, but no figures were given to back this up and it was not the case.

# References

Andrews, C.L. (1979) Tenants and Town Hall, HMSO, London

CHAC (1969) *Council Housing, Purposes, Procedures and Priorities: Ninth Report*, HMSO, London

Cohen, D.K. (1975) "The Value of Social Experiments" in *Planned Variation in Education* (eds.) A. Rivlin and P.M. Timpane, Brookings Institution, Washington

Coleman, A. (1985) *Utopia on Trial*, Shipman, London.

Dept of Environment (1981 a, b, c) *An investigation into hard to let housing*, Vols 1-3, DoE, HMSO, London

Dept of Environment (1984) *Local Housing Management A Priority Estates Project*, Survey, HMSO, London

Forrest, R. and Murie, A. (1988) *Selling the Welfare State : The Privatisation of Public Housing*, Routledge, London

Hillier, B. and Hanson, J. (1984) *The Social Logic of Space*, Cambridge University Press, Cambridge

Hirsch, F. (1977) *The Social Limits to Growth*, Routledge, London

Hope, T. (1988) "Area, crime and incivility: a profile from the British Crime Survey" in (eds.) Hope, T. and Shaw, M. *Communities and Crime Reduction*, Home Office Research and Planning Unit, HMSO, London

Hope, T. and Foster, J. (1993) [details to be added]

Housing Research Group (1981) *Could local Authorities be better Landlords?*, City University, London

Jacobs, J. (1961) *The Death and Life of Great American Cities*, Random House, London

Jephcott, P. (1971) *Homes in High Flats some of the human problems involved in multi story housing*, Oliver and Boyd, Edinburgh

Mainwaring, R. (1988) *The Walsall Experience*, DoE, HMSO, London

Malpass, P. (1983) "Residualisation and the restructuring of housing tenure", *Housing Review*, 32, p44-45

Malpass, P. and Murie, A. *Housing Policy and Practice*, Macmillan, (1987) Basingstoke

Minford, P.et al (1987) *The Housing Morass*, Institute of Economic Affairs, London

NACRO (1982) *Neighbourhood Consultations - a Practical Guide*, National Association for the Care and Rehabilitation of Offenders, London

Newman, O. (1972) *Defensible Space*, Macmillan, London

Power, A. (1984) *Local Housing Management: A Priority Estates Project Survey*, DoE, HMSO, London (op cit DoE above)

Power, A. (1987) *Property before People*, Allen and Unwin, London

Power, A. (1987) "The crisis in council housing: is public housing mananagable?", Discussion Paper WSP/21, Welfare State Programme, LSE; also in *LSE Quarterly*, Spring 1988

Power, A. (1991) *Housing Management: a guide to quality and creativity*, Longmans, London

Priority Estates *The PEP Guide to Local Housing Management*, Vols 1-3, Project (1987) DoE, HMSO, London

Rivlin A.(1971) *Systematic Thinking for Social Action*, Brookings Institution, Washington

Teymur, N. et al (1988) *Rehumanising Housing*, Butterworths, London

Timpane, P.M.(1970) "Educational Experimentation in National Social Policy", *Harvard Educational Review*, Vol 40, pp 560-62

Wilson, J.J. (1987) *The Truely Disadvantaged*

Wilson, J.J. (1991) "Research and the Truly Disadvantaged", in *The Urban Underclass*, Brookings Institution, Washington

Wilson, S. (1978) "Updating Defensible Space", *Architects Journal*, 11 October

Wilson, S. (1980) "Vandalism and Defensible Space on London Housing Estates", in (eds.) R. Clarke and P. Mughen, *Designing out Crime*, HMSO, London

| | |
|---|---|
| *Appendix* | Research design and method |

**Overall research design**

The designed conformed as nearly as possible to the standard randomised control trial procedure. The two pairs of estates were matched for size, location, housing design and social mix. Comparable information was collected, both before and after PEP intervention, over a three year period. The first stage of the Home Office funded tenant survey was undertaken **before** the estate offices were opened in June 1987. The second tenant survey was mounted in June 1990.

There were four main objectives to the housing element in the project.

**1 Monitor the management change**

The ten component parts of PEP's strategy for estate based management were regularly compared to the actual arrangements made on each experimental site. The research officer visited the sites monthly and both observed practice and interviewed managers.

**2 Monitor housing management performance**

The project developed performance indicators of standards of housing management drawing on previous work by the Audit Commission and PEP itself. The measures were applied before and after the opening of the estate offices on the experimental sites and after the comparable period in the control estates. These measures relied on the administrative records kept by the local authorities but involved extensive cross checking of different original sources to test their reliability. A detailed description of the sources used and the problems encountered is given below.

**3 Environmental standards indicators**

The project developed quantitative measures of the environmental standards on the estates that was to be repeated at three monthly intervals throughout the three year period. These included damage to property and the condition and cleanliness of common areas. These statistical indicators were supplemented by photographic evidence from standard viewing points on the estate, collected at the same time as the environmental survey. This survey method is described in detail below.

**4 Evaluating the management process**

This involved regular observation in the local office, in depth semi-structured interviews with key staff and other participants such as councillors and tenants' representatives. The objective was to build up a more qualitative understanding of the dynamics of management change and the difficulties and opportunities as they were perceived by those involved.

**The environmental survey methodology**
Purpose

The main purpose of the survey was to measure as objectively as possible the quality of the environment tenants experienced over the period of the study. The second purpose was to incorporate measures that outsiders might consider important in classifying the estate. Tenants' subjective assessments had been surveyed in the Tenant Survey but their expectations could change and it was thought important to have some independent check on actual phenomena.

The essential problem was to objectify as intangible a concept as the quality of the environment and to capture those items reflecting the criminological literature on vandalism and incivilities. We were able to draw on the work of Alice Coleman who had sought to do something similar (Coleman 1985).

It was decided to begin with the tenants' own judgements about their quality of life. They were asked in tenant survey in June 1987 what they considered to be "a big problem" on the estates. Those responses that related to the physical environment were taken and, where possible, a measure was created to monitor tenants' concerns. This was not always easy. We included excrement in lifts, stairways and balconies as objectionable evidence of dogs but this only captured part of tenants' concern. Broken lights on stairways at night were a cause of complaint but it was decided it would be impractical to conduct night time surveys. The items listed by tenants mostly included those referred to in the criminological literature. Listed in order of importance given by tenants, the environmental nuisances were:

> Rubbish and litter lying around
>
> Dogs
>
> Graffiti
>
> Broken windows
>
> Broken doors
>
> Dirty communal areas i.e. stairs, hallways, lifts
>
> Empty houses and flats
>
> Secure car parking

**Defining the space**

It was decided to distinguish areas according to Oscar Newman's (1972) categories: private space, semi-private space, semi-public and public space. It was necessary to adapt these categories to the kind of architecture found on the four estates. The space was defined as follows:

Private space | Private garden, balcony used by one dwelling, doors and windows of a dwelling

Semi-private | A lift lobby shared by a small number of dwellings, shared access to a balcony by no more than four dwellings

Semi-public | Common staircases, deck access

Public | Open areas, forecourts, playing areas

**Creating the measures**

The items had to be described clearly enough to be repeatable by other research workers than the ones who designed the survey. It was also decided that it was insufficient for our purposes to merely ask the researcher to record the existence of graffiti or rubbish. This would have produced too insensitive an indicator to pick up changes over time. Scores from 0-5 were experimented with. The wider range had some advantages but it was difficult to administer. The most practical proved to be 0-3 in most cases.

It was felt better to avoid the use of terms like "vandalism" and to merely ask the researcher to record the scale of damage which could have been the result of wind damage, over use, accident or other non perjoritative reasons. All the blocks or areas in the experimental estates were sampled for observation and half the areas or blocks in the control estates. Each chosen block was divided into small areas. Each sub area had a code corresponding to the geographical code adopted by the Home Office in categorising the areas in which crimes occurred. This made it possible to relate changes in these indicators of damage and abuse to trends in crime. These areas could be also be grouped in ways that corresponded to units recognisable to tenants - blocks of flats or "Thorpes" in Hull. Each experimental estate had roughly 150 observation sites.

**Validation**

Since the measures were to some extent subjective it was important to see if independent observers produced similar results. Two researchers from the Home Office who were not practised in using the survey were asked to administer it "cold". Their results produced raw scores for the whole estate that came within 5% of the experienced researcher in the case of public and semi-public areas but a little more on the semi-private areas where there were fewer observations. The observations of the private areas were almost identical. In fact, all the observations were undertaken by the same experienced research worker throughout the study. There was thus no variation between scores due to inter-rater variability. Scores for areas on which local people said no changes had occurred that they were aware of, vary by no more than 1 or 2 percent in the study period. This suggests that the survey method was fairly robust.

**Creating an index**

By adding all the maximum possible scores together for all areas or for one sub-area it is possible to produce a maximum potential raw score. Then an actual score can be produced for each area and the actual score expressed as a percentage of the potential score. A score of 100 would mean that every part of a given site sampled was covered in serious rubbish with large areas of graffiti, seriously broken walls, broken windows, faeces in the common areas, communal doors damaged, rubbish chutes blocked, dry risers broken and garages broken too. That would suggest an environment of some considerable squalor. The fact that some flats scored 50 at some points is a sad commentary on their environment.

There were many possible ways to present this data. The simplest was to aggregate all the raw scores and arrive at an average "incivilities score". The total potential score on the London experimental estate, for example, was 6850. Because of the way the scoring had been designed, however, the weight of the scoring varied between different types of damage. Since the areas for graffiti and rubbish were so great they had large raw scores and broken communal doors had lower total potential scores. On the London experimental estates 42% of the total potential raw scores relate to rubbish, for example. In Hull the figure was 39%. We might not want to assign a weight of 40% to rubbish in our overall assessment. There seemed to be two ways of handling this problem. One was to show each phenomenon separately. This would mean a separate measure for graffiti, rubbish and no overall average that subsumed the very different kinds of damage. This is least unsatisfactory but it can make the picture difficult to assimilate. The other and complementary method was to weight each form of abuse equally or to take the main forms of abuse - rubbish, graffiti, damage to buildings in some form and then take together all other forms of damage or litter on open areas, broken fences and the like. Each four groups of abuse were then given equal weights to create the "average" indicator of abuse.

**The variables**

Actual scores

AVAR 1    All rubbish

AVAR 2    All graffiti

AVAR 3    Internal property damage

AVAR 4    Windows broken or boarded up

AVAR 5    Dwelling boarded up

AVAR 6    External property damage

AVAR 7    Grass open space damage or litter

AVAR 8    Garages or sheds damage

AVAR 9    New fence damage graffiti

These are repeated for potential scores

PAVR 1    etc

The reduced list includes AVAR 1 - AVAR 3 while the fourth variable is a combination of AVAR 4 - AVAR 9. Each is given an equal weight to produce the average.

Printed in the United Kingdom for HMSO.
Dd.0297248, 11/93, C12, 3396/4, 5673, 263792.